BUTTONS IN SETS
1896 - 1972

by

Marshall N. Levin & Theodore L. Hake

Published by
Hake's Americana & Collectibles Press
P.O. Box 1444 • York, PA 17405

ACKNOWLEDGMENTS

Our warmest thanks to these collectors across the country who helped with details on the listings in this volume; we appreciate their patience and willingness to share their expertise:

WILLIAM ALBRIGHT
GARY AZERIER
KEN CHAPMAN
TOM COLLIER
ED EVERS
RALPH GRABER
JACK HOLLAND
RUSSELL KING
WALTER KOENIG
DAVID LUEBKE
HY MANDELOWITZ
FOSTER POLLACK

EDWARD POTTER
STEVEN RAZUM
KEITH SCHNEIDER
PAUL SENSIBAUGH
BRUCE AND PAT SHELTON
PHIL SHIMKIN
SHIRLEY SMITH
TOM SONNENBERG
JOHN STAFFORD
ROGER STECKLER
MIKE WEST
JOHN WINGERT

ISBN 0-918708-04-4

INTRODUCTION

Buttons have been issued in sets and series ever since the first celluloid pin-backs were manufactured in the 1890's. Indeed, the "series" antedate the pinbacks, since many of the early sets of celluloid buttons were simply an expression, in a new medium, of previous series of trade cards, tobacco silks, insert cards, etc. These had been collected avidly and widely, both in the United States and abroad, and it wasn't long before pinback buttons joined other collections as a serious hobby for Victorian gentlemen and ladies.

The first of these buttons—7/8" celluloids—were issued primarily by cigarette and gum manufacturers, most notably Sweet Caporal and American Pepsin. The buttons, packaged with the product, were colorful, topical, historical, well designed, well made, and free. Set followed set in endless profusion—actresses, baseball players, flags, the Yellow Kid, poets and presidents, ships, jockeys, snappy sayings, flowers, Indians, and on and on. They amused, instructed, enter-tained, and—we may be sure—sold the product. And they were collected. In the years since, buttons in sets have been produced on practically every subject imaginable.

This volume is an attempt to catalog these sets of buttons, from the first to the early 1970's. It is not a complete listing—at this late date a complete listing may no longer be possible. But we have started cataloguing additional sets for future volumes and we would welcome word of any sets or individual buttons we may have missed.

Listings of sets has been organized for ease of reference—first by broad categories (comics, sports, etc.), then, within each category, either by issuer (Kellogg's Pep, Sweet Caporal, etc.) or by subject (Mickey Mouse, The Wizard of Oz, etc.). The index offers a quick means of locating specific sets, subjects or issuers.

Note: Information for each set is given in this sequence as far as possible: Issuing Company. Date issued or approximate era. Size and type of button. Colors. Name of manufacturer. Additonal pertinent descriptions. Number of buttons in set, when known, or number seen and verified. And, finally, a listing of the individual buttons that comprise the set. Minor varieties of the same button may be mentioned but are not counted in totals. Major varieties, however, indicative of separate printings, are counted separately. Incorrect spellings, inconsistencies in punctuation, abbreviations, etc., are copied from the buttons themselves—except when they are our own mistakes.

ABBREVIATIONS

BW	black and white
CELL	celluloid
I.U.	issuer unknown
LITHO	lithograph
MC	multicolor
W&H	Whitehead & Hoag

CONTENTS

AIRPLANES

BOND BREAD

Bond Bread. 1930's. 1¼" cell. BW and one color. Bastian. Two numbered series of 6 each: one series with advertising copy in top segment, the other around top rim. Planes are identical except #4. **Numbered set of 12.**

1 LINDBERGH'S "SPIRIT OF ST. LOUIS"
2 POST and GATTY'S "WINNIE MAE"
3 COMMANDER BYRD'S "FLOYD BENNETT"
4 AUTOGYRO

4 COSTE AND BELLONTE'S "QUESTION MARK"
5 AMELIA EARHART'S "FRIENDSHIP"
6 FLOYD BENNETT'S "JOSEPHINE FORD"

KELLOGG'S PEP

Kellogg's Pep. 1940's. 1⅛" litho. Brown, blue and white. No mfr. 11 seen.

BOEING B-29 SUPERFORTRESS
CONSOLIDATED PB2Y-3 CORONADO
  (2 diff.)
CONSOLIDATED VULTEE B-24 LIBERATOR
GRUMMAN F6F3 HELLCAT

LOCKHEED LIGHTNING (P-38)
MARTIN B-26 MARAUDER (2 diff.)
NORTH AMERICAN B-25 MITCHELL
  (2 diff.)
REPUBLIC P-47 THUNDERBOLT

YANK JUNIOR

Yank Junior (Clothing). 1930's. 13/16" litho. MC. No mfr. 19 seen.

ADMIRAL BYRD'S SOUTH POLE PLANE
BELLANCA BOMBER
BOEING ARMY BIPLANE P-12-E
BOEING ARMY PURSUIT PLANE P-26-A
BOEING BOMBER
CAPT. RICKENBACKERS 12 HOUR COAST
  TO COAST PLANE
CARIBBEAN CLIPPER - S42
COLONEL CHAS. A. LINDBERGH'S SPIRIT
  OF ST. LOUIS
CONDOR 155 BIPLANE
FIRST EAST TO WEST TRANSATLANTIC
  PLANE JUNKERS W33

FIRST ENGLAND TO AUSTRALIA PLANE
  WHITTELSEY AVIAN
FIRST WRIGHT BIPLANE - 1903
FOKKER F32 ADMIRAL BYRD'S NORTH
  POLE PLANE
FORD TRI-MOTORED TRANSPORT
GRAF ZEPPLIN
LARGEST AIR LINER CLIPPER SHIP - No. 5
MARTIN BOMBER
NAVY CURTISS RACING SEAPLANE
WORLD'S FASTEST TRANSPORT VULTEE
  41-A 215 M.P.H.

JET PLANES

Issuer Unknown. 1950's. 1″ litho. MC. No mfr. (MADE IN U.S.A. on curl.) **Set of 12.**

B-47 STRATOJET
B-57 NIGHT INTRUDER
BELL X-1A
CONVAIR XF-92
D-558 SKYROCKET
DOUGLAS SKYSTREAK

F7U CUTLASS
F-86D SABRE
F-88 VOODOO
F9F-6 COUGAR
F-94C STARFIRE
XF4D-SKYRAY

PLANES & PILOTS

Issuer Unknown. 1930's. 13/16″ litho. BW on one color. Greenduck. **Numbered set of 70.**

1 EARLY PLANE "PUSHER" TYPE
2 DR. RUMPLER'S TAUBE GERMAN 1911
3 WORLD WAR ALBATROS D-3 VON RICHTHOFEN'S FIGHTER
4 HAWKER "NIMROD"
5 PTERODACTYL II TAILLESS PLANE
6 BOEING 40 B-4
7 FOKKER TRANSPORT F-32
8 TRAVEL-AIR'S "MYSTERY SHIP"
9 GILMORE "RECORD BREAKER"
10 ART CHESTER'S RACER
11 CAPRONI 114
12 U.S. NAVY FIGHTER CURTISS HAWK
13 WACO SEAPLANE
14 FLYING BOAT
15 SEVERSKY AMPHIBION
16 FORD TRI-MOTOR
17 BLERIOT 290 MODERN "PUSHER"
18 BOEING 247-D UNITED AIR LINES
19 DOUGLAS DC-2 AMERICAN AIRLINES
20 "CHINA CLIPPER" PAN AMERICAN AIRWAYS
21 "ZEPHIR" - GERMAN 1936 TRANS-ATLANTIC FLYING BOAT
22 MARTIN B-10 BOMBER AMERICAN 1936
23 DOUGLAS O-38 B OLD ARMY TRAINER - AMERICAN
24 NEW DOUGLAS O-43 ARMY OBSERVATION - AMERICAN
25 NAVY "HELLDIVER" CURTISS SHIPBOARD FIGHTER 1931
26 4 PASS. PRIVATE BIPLANE WACO CUSTOM CABIN CRUISER 1936
27 ITALIAN "TRICAP" PURSUIT PLANE
28 WILEY POST'S "WINNIE MAE" 'ROUND THE WORLD 1933
29 BLERIOT'S MONO PLANE FIRST FLEW ENGLISH CHANNEL 1909
30 FAMED WRIGHT BROTHERS' "PUSHER" PLANE
31 ORVILLE WRIGHT - AMERICAN FIRST MAN TO FLY
32 GLENN CURTISS - AMERICAN AVIATION PIONEER
33 LOUIS BLERIOT - FRENCH FIRST FLEW ENGLISH CHANNEL

34 ARCH HOXSEY EARLY TEST PILOT
35 EUGENE ELY - IN PIONEER PILOT'S "CRASH HELMET"
36 HARRY HAWKER - BRITISH EARLY DISTANCE PILOT
37 CAPT. EDDIE RICKENBACKER AMERICAN WAR ACE
38 MAJOR REED G. LANDIS AMERICAN WAR ACE
39 LIEUT. OAKLEY KELLY BELOVED AMERICAN PILOT
40 COL. CHARLES A. LINDBERG FIRST TRANS-ATLANTIC SOLO MAY 21, 1927
41 CLARENCE D. CHAMBERLIN NEW YORK TO GERMANY WITH LEVINE - JUNE 6, 1927
42 GEORGE HALDEMAN ENDURANCE FLYER
43 EDDIE STINSON ENDURANCE FLYER
44 COL. ARTHUR C. GOEBLE VETERAN PILOT
45 CAPT. LOWELL H. SMITH - COMMANDER AMERICAN 'ROUND THE WORLD FLIGHT
46 LIEUT. LEIGH WADE - CREW MEMBER AMERICAN 'ROUND THE WORLD FLIGHT
47 CAPT. KINGSFORD-SMITH - BRITISH PILOT "SOUTHERN CROSS"
48 CAPT. T.P. ULM - BRITISH CO-PILOT "SOUTHERN CROSS"
49 DICK GRACE MOVIE "CRASH PILOT"
50 JIMMY HAIZLIP DISTANCE PILOT
51 "SPEED" HOLMAN RACING PILOT
52 JOE CROSSON ALASKAN RESCUE PILOT
53 BOUSSOTROT FRENCH AIR HERO
54 MAURICE ROSSI - FRENCH N.Y. TO SYRIA NONSTOP WITH PAUL CODOS - 1933
55 LIEUT. RICHARD ATCHERLEY BRITISH RACING PILOT
56 "CASEY" JONES VETERAN RACING PILOT
57 CAPT. FRANK HAWKS VETERAN COAST-TO-COAST FLYER
58 CAPT. A.W. STEVENS HIGH ALTITUDE AIR PHOTOGRAPHER
59 JAMES MATTERN N.Y. TO BERLIN NONSTOP WITH GRIFFIN - 1931
60 BENNET GRIFFIN N.Y. TO BERLIN NONSTOP WITH MATTERN - 1931
61 CLYDE PANGBORN VETERAN PILOT
62 COL. ROSCOE TURNER RACING PILOT
63 JACK KNIGHT - UNITED AIR LINES "MILLION MILES" PILOT
64 HOWARD HUGHES COAST-TO-COAST NONSTOP RECORD BREAKER
65 JIMMY COLLINS BELOVED AMERICAN TEST PILOT
66 LOMA WORTH WOMAN STUNT PILOT
67 "BOBBIE" TROUT WOMAN TRANSPORT PILOT
68 RUTH NICHOLS VETERAN WOMAN PILOT
69 AMY JOHNSON - BRITISH WOMAN DISTANCE PILOT
70 AMELIA EARHART PUTMAN 1st WOMAN TRANS-ATLANTIC SOLO FLIGHT -
   MAY 21, 1923

ANIMALS/BIRDS

ANIMALS

American Pepsin Gum. Circa 1900. 7/8″ cell. MC. W&H. 17 seen.

BEAR
BLACK BASS
BUFFALO
COCKER SPANIEL.*
ELEPHANT.
ELK*
ENGLISH SETTER.
GIRAFFE.
GREY FOX

LION.
MEXICAN HAIRLESS.**
MONKEY.
SUNOL RACE HORSE
SUNOL, RACE HORSE*
SUNOL, RACE HORSE.
TIGER.
ZEBRA.

*Color variety seen.
**Four varieties seen.

BIRDS

American Pepsin Gum. Circa 1900. 7/8″ cell. MC. W&H. Issued in two distinct series, one with more black in the drawings. (d) means button was seen only in dark series; (1) means button was seen only in light series. Others were seen in both series. 38 seen.

BALTIMORE ORIOL (d)
BALTIMORE ORIOLE. (1)
BLUE BIRD.
BLUE BUNTING.
BLUE JAY. (1)
BOB O LINK (d)
BOB-O-LINK (1)
CANARY.
CUCKOO.
EAGLE.
FANTAIL PIGEON.
GAME ROOSTER
HORNED OWL.

HUMMING BIRD. (1)
KINGFISHER. (1)
MAGPIE. (1)
MOCKING BIRD.
ROBIN. (1)
SEA GULL (d)
SNOW BIRD.
SPARROW. (1)*
WHIP-POOR-WILL.
WOODPECKER.
WOOD THRUSH. (1)
WREN.

*Also seen in tin frame, 15/16″, long-shank pin, with no issuer identification.

BIRDS

Issuer Unknown. 1930's. 13/16" litho. MC. No mfr., except as noted. Seen with both silver and gold backs, with minor color variations. **Set of 40.**

BARN OWL
BARN SWALLOW
BLUEBIRD
BLUE JAY
BOBOLINK
CARDINAL
CATBIRD
CHICKADEE
FLICKER
GOLDFINCH
GREEN JAY
INDIGO BUNTING
KING BIRD
KINGFISHER
MAGPIE
MEADOWLARK
MOCKING BIRD
ORIOLE
PAINTED BUNTING
PELICAN

PHEASANT*
PHOEBE
PURPLE MARTIN
QUAIL (BOBWHITE)
RED HEADED WOODPECKER
RED-WINGED BLACKBIRD
ROBIN
ROSE-BREASTED GROSBEAK
SANDPIPER
SCARLET TANAGER
SONG SPARROW
SUMMER TANAGER
SWAN
WESTERN TANAGER
WHITE-WINGED CROSSBILL
WILD DUCK
WOOD THRUSH
WREN
YELLOW BELLIED SAPSUCKER
YELLOW WARBLER

Also seen with Geraghty logo on back.

DOGS

Issuer Unknown. 1930's. 13/16" litho. MC. No mfr., except as noted. **Set of 35.**

AFGHAN
AIREDALE
BLOODHOUND
BOSTON TERRIER
BULL TERRIER
CAIRN*
CHOW
COCKER SPANIEL
COLLIE
DACHSHUND
DALMATIAN
DOBERMAN PINSCHER
ENGLISH BULL
ESKIMO HUSKIE
FOX TERRIER
GREAT DANE
GREYHOUND
IRISH TERRIER

NEWFOUNDLAND*
PEKINGESE
POINTER
POLICE DOG
POMERANIAN
POODLE
PUG DOG
SAINT BERNARD
SCHIPPERKE
SCOTTISH TERRIER
SETTER
SHEEP DOG
SPITZ
SPRINGER SPANIEL
WIRE FOX TERRIER
WOLF HOUND
YORKSHIRE TERRIER

Geraghty logo on back.

DOGS, CHAMPIONS

Issuer Unknown. 1930's. 7/8" litho. MC. Cruver. 43 seen.

AFGHAN DOG "DORTEN GAITER"
AIREDALE TERRIER "SHELTEROCK MISTER SPOTLIGHT"
AMERICAN GERMAN POLICE DOG "AMERICA'S BEAUTY"
BASSET HOUND "RUDEL DE-EL"
BORDER TERRIER "ROBERT OF TYL"
BORZOI "SULAN OF GREEN"
BOXER "DORIAN VON MARIENHOF"
CANADIAN AIREDALE "TORO OF CANS"
CHIHUAHUA "BEBITA OF ORO"
CHOW "CHIA-WAN'S RED MONARCH"
COLLIE "GERONINE GREY JACKET II"
COLORED BULL TERRIER "JEHANNE OF NIGHT RIDERS"*
DALMATIAN "CREEL OF EDGEWOOD"
DOBERMANN PINSCHER "SIEGLINDE V. HEIDLEBERG"
ENGLISH BULLDOG "MERGER ODD WAN"
ENGLISH HOUND DOG "DEL OF LEE"
ENGLISH SHEEPDOG "ALICE GRUESVERGEN OF ENGLAND"
ENGLISH WHIPPET "WELSH REEVER"
FOX TERRIER "RED FOX"
FOX TERRIER "SINKA ESTA"
GERMAN SHEPHERD "BLITTEN FRUM GELSTENT"
GERMAN SHEPHERD "NASH OF BEACH CLIFF"

GORDON SETTER "TROYDEL"
GREAT DANE "BEREN"
GREAT PYRENEES "BASGRAIRE FLEURETTE"
GREYHOUND "CHASE BOY OF GADS"
IRISH SETTER "NEWTONARDS ARISTOCRAT"
IRISH TERRIER "CLYDE OF TREMAINE"
IRISH WOLFHOUND "LE MAXER"
JAPANESE SPANIEL "MELIC, KING OF THE SPANIELS"
KEESHONDEN "RUTHERFORD'S DELIGHT"
KERRY BLUE TERRIER "SKIPP'S DELIGHT
LABRADOR RETRIEVER "BANCHORY TRUMP OF WINGAN"
MINIATURE SCHNAUZER "JEFF OF WALLATON"
SAMOYEDE "TIPSI DER VERBEN"
SEALYHAM "ST. MARGARET OF HILLS"
SPRINGER SPANIEL "MARTHA GREENSIDE"
WELSH CORGI PEMBROKE "SIERRA BOWHIT PIRAT"
WELSH TERRIER "KID ROCK"
WHIPPET "BEAUTY'S PRIDE"
WHITE BEDLINGTON "ROSEMONT"
WHITE SEALYHAM TERRIER "ALISON'S GUARD"
WIRE-HAIRED TERRIER "DELTAH OF MI TOO"

Also seen without Cruver logo.

COMICS

COMIC CARTOONS

Hassan and Tokio Cigarettes (also seen with W&H paper). Circa 1912. 7/8″ cell. Issued in various printings: multicolor, black and white, white on blue, and white on red. Mfr'd mainly by W&H, some by Ehrman and T. J. Gleason. Cartoonists include Rube Goldberg, TAD, Hal Hoffman, Bud Fisher, George Herriman, George McManus, Tom McNamara, Rudolph Dirks, TEP, Gus Mager, HBM, C.M. Payne. Sometimes the same cartoon was used with different sayings, and vice versa. More than 290 MC and 170 BW seen.

COMIC CARTOONS

Issuer Unknown. Circa 1910. 1¼″ litho. MC. No mfr. (Buttons have "Factory No. 30. 2nd District New York" on reverse. Both Hassan and Sweet Caporal Cigarettes have been identified with this tobacco factory, but it is not known at this time who issued this series.) Cartoonists include Bud Fisher, Rube Goldberg, TAD. 48 seen.

A BOOB IS AN AWFUL THING
ALL TO THE MUSTARD
BEAT IT! (2 diff.)
CAN IT!
CURTAINS FOR YOU
CUT THAT STUFF
DON'T SAY IT JUST WINK
DON'T YOU LOVE ME NO MO?
EH?
EVERYBODY'S DOIN IT
GONE BUT NOT FORGOTTEN
GOOD NIGHT
HELLO BILL
I GOT CHA STEVE (2 diff.)
I'LL TAKE THE SAME
I'M STUCK ON YOU
I'M THE GUY!
I'M THE GUY THAT DONE IT ALL
I RAISE YOU
I SHOULD WORRY
I'VE GOT A PAIR OF QUEENS
I'VE GOT YOUR NUMBER
KEEP OFF THE GRASS
KISS ME, NOTHING MAKES ME SICK

LEAD ME TO IT
LET'S SEE WHAT YOU'VE GOT
NOBODY LOVES A FAT MAN
NOT ON YOUR LIFE
NOW WILL YOU BE GOOD
OH WHAT I'D DO FOR A CHICKEN LIKE
   YOU
OH YOU CUBS
ON YOUR WAY
SHE CAN PUT HER SUGAR IN MY
   COFFEE
SHE'S A BEAR
SPEAK RIGHT OUT
STRUCK WITH DELIGHT
TAKE IT FROM ME, BO.
TAKE THAT NOISE OUTSIDE
TELL IT TO SWEENY
THIS IS ON ME
TIE THAT BULL OUTSIDE
TWICE IN THE SAME PLACE
WATCH YOUR STEP
WHO WISHED THIS ON ME
YOU POOR BOOB
YOURS IN HASTE

COMIC SAYINGS

These early buttons seem to have been the province of the cigarette companies, possibly because of the daring of some of the humor—**O.U. Chicken!; Tickle Me; Am I The First; Mamie, Come Kiss Your Honey Boy;** and so on. Anyway, we have found only one non-tobacco company, Faultless Gum, that issued these sayings buttons, along with Perfection Cigarette, Sweet Caporal, High Admiral, Clix, Chesterfield, Obak, Favorite, Picayune, and American Oval Crimped Seal Cigarettes, and Red Lion Plug Tobacco. Most are 7/8" cell., but 13/16" and 31/32" celluloids with filled backs also appear, as well as a 1¼" litho set by Perfection. High Admiral also issued a series in German. All were two colors, either white on red, blue or green, or different colored type on white. They apparently enjoyed two periods of great popularity, first in the 1890's and again around 1912. Mfrs. include W&H, Phelps & Sons, Thos. Jay Gleason, Baldwin & Gleason, General Mfg. Co., and Aluminum Novelty Co. Including color varieties, more than 500 have been seen.

COMIC SWEATERS

Unknown Sweater Co. 1930's. 1¼" cell. MC. Parisian Novelty Co. 6 seen.

BOOTS AND HER BUDDIES	ORPHAN ANNIE (side view)
JUST KIDS	SKEEZIX
ORPHAN ANNIE (head & shoulders)	SMITTY

COMIC TOGS

Comic Togs. 1945-1947. Similar to Kellogg's Pep set on page 10. 13/16" litho. MC. No mfr. Three varieties of rim inscriptions: 1) COPR. 1945 FAMOUS ARTISTS SYN. 2) COPR. 1946 KING FEATURES SYN. INC. 3) COPR. 1947 FAMOUS ARTISTS SYN. 12 seen.

ANDY GUMP*	PA WINKLE*
BLONDIE DAGWOOD	PERRY DIMWIT
DICK TRACY*	POPEYE*
HERBY SMITTY	STEVE CANYON
JOE PALOOKA	THE KATZENJAMMER KIDS
ORPHAN ANNIE*	TINY TIM

*Same design as in Kellogg's Pep set.

JUST KIDS SAFETY CLUB

Various Newspapers. 1930's. 1¼'' cell. MC. W&H, Bastian and Offset Gravure. Issued with different comic characters by various newspapers. Some have been seen without newspaper identification. Since many of these buttons carry different illustrations, we have described them in detail. Left and right in the descriptions are from the observer's point of view. Profile means only one eye is shown and 3/4 face means both eyes are shown. 11 characters/18 picture variations/42 newspapers seen.

CHARACTERS

BAGEARS (walking left)
FATSO (3 diff: walking right profile; walking right 3/4 face; facing left)
GRANPOP (on roller skates moving left)
MARJORY (3 diff: walking left 3/4 face; walking right profile in two different size pictures)
MOM (facing right)
MUSH (2 diff; walking left; running right)
NICODEMUS (2 diff: walking right in two different sizes)
OFFICER BRANNER* (walking left)
PEANUT (walking left)
POP (facing right)
SERAPHIN O'TOOLE (swinging fist to right)

*Inscription on the button issued by THE RECORD says SERGEANT BRANNER and has subtle differences in the drawing.

NEWSPAPERS

ALBANY TIMES UNION
ANDERSON HERALD
ATLANTIC NEWS-TELEGRAPH
CHICAGO AMERICAN
CINCINNATI TIMES-STAR
CLEVELAND PLAIN DEALER
DEFIANCE CRESCENT-NEWS
DELPHOS HERALD
DETROIT TIMES
EVENING EXPRESS
LOCKPORT UNION-SUN & JOURNAL
MARION STAR
NASSAU DAILY REVIEW
NEW BRITAIN DAILY HERALD
NEW HAVEN REGISTER
NEW YORK EVENING JOURNAL
N.Y. EVENING JOURNAL
OAKLAND POST ENQUIRER
OSKALOOSA DAILY HERALD
PITTSBURGH SUN-TELEGRAPH
PLAINFIELD COURIER-NEWS

POST INTELLIGENCER
SYRACUSE JOURNAL
TARANAKI HERALD
THE DAILY REPORTER
THE DAILY STAR
THE DAILY TIMES
THE DENVER POST
THE DETROIT TIMES
THE EVENING JOURNAL
THE FREMONT MESSENGER
THE GLOBE
THE HONOLULU ADVERTISER
THE LIMA NEWS
THE PEEKSKILL STAR
THE RECORD
THE SAN DIEGO UNION
THE TIMES
THE WILLIAMSPORT SUN
URBANA DAILY CITIZEN
WICHITA BEACON
WISCONSIN NEWS

KELLOGG'S PEP

Kellogg's Pep. 1945-1947. 13/16'' litho. MC. No mfr. (Copyright King Features Syn. Inc.; Famous Artists Syn.; or D.C. Inc.) Three varieties of back: 1) Kellogg's Pep 2) MADE IN U.S.A. Kellogg's Pep 3) Blank. **Set of 86.**

ABRETHA BREEZE	HERBY	RIP WINKLE
ANDY GUMP	INSPECTOR	SANDY
AUNTIE BLOSSOM	JIGGS	SHADOW
BARNEY GOOGLE	JUDY	SKEEZIX
BEEZIE	JUNIOR TRACY	SMILIN' JACK
BLONDIE	KAYO	SMITTY
B.O. PLENTY	LILLUMS	SMOKEY STOVER
BRENDA STARR	LITTLE JOE	SNUFFY SMITH
CASPER	LITTLE KING	SPUD
CHESTER GUMP	LITTLE MOOSE	SUPERMAN
CHIEF BRANDON	LORD PLUSHBOTTOM	TESS TRUEHEART
CINDY	MAC	THE CAPTAIN
CORKY	MAGGIE	THE FIRE CHIEF
DAGWOOD	MAMA DE STROSS	THE PHANTOM
DAISY	MAMA KATZENJAMMER	TILDA
DENNY	MAMIE	TILLIE THE TOILER
DICK TRACY	MA WINKLE	TINY TIM
DON WINSLOW	MIN GUMP	TOOTS
EMMY	MOON MULLINS	UNCLE AVERY
FAT STUFF	MR. BAILEY	UNCLE BIM
FELIX THE CAT	MR. BIBBS	UNCLE WALT
FLASH GORDON	NINA	UNCLE WILLIE
FLATTOP	OLIVE OYL	VITAMIN FLINTHEART
FRITZ	ORPHAN ANNIE	WARBUCKS
GOOFY	PAT PATTEN	WILMER
GRAVEL GERTIE	PERRY WINKLE	WIMPY
HANS	POPEYE	WINNIE'S TWINS
HAROLD TEEN	POP JENKS	WINNIE WINKLE
HENRY	PUNJAB	

KING FEATURES

King Features Syndicate. 1930's. 13/16'' litho. MC. Parisian Novelty Co. 7 seen.

DALE ARDEN
FLASH GORDON
JEEP

LITTLE ANNIE ROONIE
OLIVE OYL

POPEYE
WIMPY

LITTLE PINKIES

American Pepsin Gum. Circa 1896. 7/8'' cell. MC. W&H. 21 seen.

BOY ORATOR.
GREENIE.
JUST LANDED.*
THE ACTOR.†
THE BAD BOY.
THE BALL PLAYER
THE BALL PLAYER.

THE BOOT BLACK. SHINE.
THE CLOWN.*
THE COLONEL.
THE DRUM MAJOR.* †
THE DUDE.
THE DUNCE.
THE FIREMAN.†

THE LETTER CARRIER.* †
THE NEWS BOY. EXTRA!
THE POLICEMAN.*
THE SAILOR.†
THE SOLDIER. (2 diff.)
UNCLE SAM.

Also issued by Old Gold Cigarette.
†Also seen in tin frame, 15/16'', long-shank pin, with no issuer identification.*

MICKEY MOUSE

Mickey Mouse Globe Trotters. 1937. 1¼'' cell. BW & red. No mfr. (Kay Kamen imprint on backpaper.) 24 seen.

BELL'S SUPER SOFT BREAD
DRINK MORE MEYER MILK DAILY
EAT DUTCH OVEN BREAD
EAT FIRCH'S MA-MADE BREAD
EAT 5 POINT BREAD
EAT Freihofer's PERFECT LOAF
EAT MIAMI MAID BREAD
EAT MORE GOLD CUP BREAD
EAT MORE HAPPY HOME BREAD
EAT MORE HOLSUM BREAD
EAT MORE KEITH'S BREAD
EAT MORE RICH-LOAF BREAD

EAT MORE SHERLOCKS BREAD
EAT N.B.C. BREAD
EAT SUNFED MY BREAD
EAT SWEANEY'S BUTTER KRUST
HALL'S GOLD PRIZE BREAD
HILL'S MASTER LOAF
I EAT N.B.C. BREAD
I EAT PETER PAN BREAD
PEVELY
STAR'S HAPPY HOME BREAD
WHITE SPONGE EXTRA
(no advertiser)

PEANUTS

Simon Simple. 1960's - 1970's. 1¾" cell. Black on one color or MC. No mfr. Copyright lines on curl are variations on United Features Syndicate, dated from 1950 to 1976. Some do not have the Simon Simple credit line. 26 seen, plus color varieties.

ALL I NEED IS ONE HIT, AND I CAN RAISE MY LIFETIME BATTING AVERAGE TO .001! (2 diff.)

BIG MAN ON THE CAMPUS! (2 diff.)

CURSE YOU, RED BARON! (RWB & black)

DOGS ACCEPT PEOPLE FOR WHAT THEY ARE..

GOOD GRIEF

HAPPY BIRTHDAY, AMERICA!! 1776-1976

HERE'S "BEAU" SNOOPY OF THE FOREIGN LEGION MARCHING ACROSS THE DESERT

I BELIEVE IN STATEHOOD, COUNTRYHOOD, CITYHOOD AND NEIGHBORHOOD!

I DON'T CARE IF ANYBODY LIKES ME . . JUST SO I'M POPULAR!

I KISSED A CRABBY FACE!

I'M ON THE MOON!

IT ALWAYS RAINS ON OUR GENERATION!

I THINK MY FEET NEED SHARPENING!

IT'S GOOD TO HAVE A FRIEND

I WONDER IF HE'S AUDITING THIS COURSE, OR TAKING IT FOR CREDIT . . .

JUST WHAT A MANAGER LIKES . . . A PLAYER WHO ISN'T BOTHERED BY TENSION!

LITTLE BROTHERS ARE THE BUCK PRIVATES OF LIFE!

SLEEPING IS AN ART

"SNOOPY, COME HOME" (MC)

SNOOPY FOR PRESIDENT (RWB)

SURF'S UP!

TO THOSE OF US WITH REAL UNDERSTANDING, DANCING IS THE ONLY PURE ART FORM!

VOTE FOR LUCY DIPLOMATIC SERVICE

YOU'RE A GOOD MAN CHARLIE BROWN

NOTE: In addition to the above cartoon buttons, there has been a multitude of 1¼" Peanuts sayings buttons, ranging from LUCY FOR FIRST LADY to SNOOPY SNIFFS AIRPLANE GLUE and appearing in many different color combinations. These are issued by many mfrs and have not been catalogued.

POGO

Issuer Unknown. 1968. 1¾'' cell. MC. No mfr.
30 seen.

A NEW BROOM BEAUTIFY OUR LAND POGO FOR PRES!
ARE WE DOWNHEARTED? LEMME THINK POGO FOR PRES
BE CRUEL TO YOUR PARENTS . . . STAY HOME   Rackety Coon
BE KIND! YOU, TOO, MAY BE A FATHER AND MOTHER SOME DAY
   Churchy La Femme
COMMIT SUTTEE . . . SMOKE IN BED   Albert
DON'T DROP OUT . . . STICK AROUND. DRIVE 'EM NUTS   Grundoon
DON'T TAKE LIFE TOO SERIOUS; IT AIN'T NOHOW PERMANENT   POGO FOR PRES
EQUAL TIME FOR POGO
FOGGY BOTTOM IS TOPLESS!   POGO for PRES
FOREIGN AFFAIRS? WE'RE FOR 'EM. POGO FOR PRES!
GOD IS NOT DEAD; HE IS MERELY UNEMPLOYED.
HEAD START PROGRAM: JUMP THE GUN! POGO FOR PRES.
IF POGO'S FOR PRESIDENT, WHO'S FOR VICE?
IF THEY WON'T DECLARE WAR, DECLARE PEACE! POGO FOR PRES
I HAVE 98.6 DEGREES FROM FAHRENHEIT U.   Howland Owl
I'LL DIG YOU IF YOU'LL DIG ME   Pogo
I'M FOR UNCIVIL RITES   POGO FOR PRES
IT'S A LONG WORM THAT HAS TO TURNING   Pogo
KEEP YOUR COOL . . . I'LL TAKE MINE HOT   Albert
LET'S GET BOMBED BEFORE WE GET BOMBED   POGO FOR PRES!
NEVER SAY NEVER   Porkypine
ON THE OTHER HAND, SUPPOSE YOU SURVIVE?   POGO FOR PRES
POGO FOR PRES!
POGO WILL <u>NOT</u> PLAY POSSUM IN THE WHITE HOUSE!
PRESIDENTIAL WORK NEATLY DONE. POGO FOR PRES
TURN ME ON   Pogo
UP THE DOWN ESCALATION! POGO FOR PRES
WE'RE ALL IN A VERY PSYCHO-DELICATE CONDITION. POGO FOR PRES
WHAT'S THE CEILING ON THE PRESI-DENSITY?
WHY & WHAT IS THE SPECIFIC GRAVITY OF THE WHITE HOUSE? POGO FOR PRES.

SNUGGLE PUP

Various Newspapers. 1923. 1⅛'' litho. BW & red.
Greenduck. Issued with different drawings by
various newspapers. 9 seen.

CALL ME CUDDLE HERALD AND EXAMINER SNUGGLE PUPS
I AM THE NEW HAVEN REGISTER SNUGGLE PUP
I AM THE NORWALK HOUR SNUGGLE PUP
I AM THE RACINE JOURNAL NEWS SNUGGLE PUP
I AM THE SAVANNAH PRESS SNUGGLE PUP
I'M A LUCKY SNUGGLE PUP HERALD AND EXAMINER
MY NAME IS JAZZ HERALD AND EXAMINER
MY NAME IS VAMP HERALD AND EXAMINER SNUGGLE PUPS
MY NAME IS TELEGRAPH SNUGGLE PUP

YELLOW KID

High Admiral/Yellow Kid Cigarettes. 1896-1898. 1¼" cell. MC with yellow rims. W&H and Riley-Klotz. **Numbered set of 155.**

There were several different printings of Yellow Kid buttons, as indicated by the variety of obverse and reverse credits. However, there are only 155 different pictures, each one numbered. Numbers 1-95 each show the Kid, usually with a saying on his nightshirt. Numbers 101-160 each show the Kid holding a different country's flag (except for 142-144). Numbers 96-100 have not been seen.

Obverse and curl credit varieties

1. HIGH ADMIRAL CIGARETTES
2. ADMIRAL CIGARETTES
3. YELLOW KID CIGARETTES
4. COPYRIGHTED 1896 OTIS F. WOOD. N.Y.
5. COPYRIGHTED 1896. B. NEUBERGER, N.Y.
6. COPYRIGHTED 1897. B. NEUBERGER, N.Y.

Reverse types and credit varieties

1. Open back, paper label with W&H patent dates or RILEY-KLOTZ M'F'G CO. UNDER W&H PATENTS
2. Tin closed back: HIGH ADMIRAL AND N.Y. JOURNAL YELLOW KID CIGARETTE
3. Tin closed back: HIGH ADMIRAL CIGARETTE
4. Tin closed back: HIGH ADMIRAL CIGARETTE YELLOW KID FLAG COLLECTION
5. Black metal closed back: HIGH ADMIRAL CIGARETTES
6. Stand-up easel back: PAT. APP'D FOR C.B.W. HIGH ADMIRAL CIGARETTE N.Y.
7. Closed back: JOURNAL'S YELLOW KID PIN-LOCK PAT'D MAY 31, '98

101 RUSSIA	121 CANADA	141 JAPAN
102 ROUMANIA	122 CUBA	142 PIRATE FLAG
103 PORTUGAL	123 PERSIA	143 AUCTION FLAG
104 NORWAY	124 IRELAND	144 RED CROSS FLAG
105 GREECE	125 SIAM	145 CHINA
106 HOLLAND	126 HONDURAS	146 MADAGASCAR
107 COSTA RICA	127 SAN DOMINGO	147 "U.S. OF COLUMBIA"*
108 GERMANY	128 FRANCE	148 SWEDEN
109 SWITZERLAND	129 SAN SALVADOR	149 BELGIUM
110 GUATAMALA	130 ARGENTINE REPUBLIC	150 PRUSSIA
111 TURKEY	131 NEW SOUTH WALES	151 ORANGE FREE STATE
112 HAYTI	132 SERVIA	152 PARAGUAY
113 AUSTRIA	133 CHILI	153 BULGARIA
114 MOROCCO	134 URUGUAY	154 LIBERIA
115 ITALY	135 MONTENEGRO •	155 PERU
116 ENGLAND	136 MEXICO	156 ECUADOR
117 BOLIVIA	137 HAWAII	157 CONGO STATE
118 VICTORIA	138 UNITED STATES	158 NICARAGUA
119 BURMAH	139 SPAIN	159 DENMARK
120 NEW ZEALAND	140 BRAZIL	160 VENEZUELA

*Also seen without quotation marks.

NEWSPAPER: EVENING LEDGER

Evening Ledger Comics (Philadelphia, Pa.). 1930's. 1¼" cell. MC. Spencer & Co. 14 seen.

BABE BUNTING
BOBBY THATCHER
CONNIE
DAN DUNN
FELIX
HAROLD TEEN
LEDGER FUN CLUB (Relentless Rudolph)

MICKEY MOUSE
MINNIE MOUSE
POPEYE
RELENTLESS RUDOLPH
SMITTY
SNUFFY SMITH
WIMPY

NEWSPAPER: JOURNAL-TRANSCRIPT

Journal-Transcript Funnies Club. 1930's. 1⅛" litho. BW. Green Duck. Characters not identified. TUNE IN WMBD around bottom. 15 seen.

CHIEF WAHOO
ELLA CINDERS
FRITZI RITZ
LITTLE ABNER (2 diff.)
MUTT & JEFF
NANCY (2 diff.)
TARZAN

UNKNOWN CHARACTER FROM CHIEF
   WAHOO STRIP
UNKNOWN COWGIRL
UNKNOWN INDIAN
UNKNOWN LITTLE GIRL
UNKNOWN MAN
UNKNOWN RABBIT

NEWSPAPER: SATURDAY CHICAGO AMERICAN

Saturday Chicago American 16 Pages of Comics. 1930's. 1" litho. MC. Greenduck. Characters not identified. 10 seen.

BETTY BOOP
BOOTS
BUCK ROGERS
FATSO
KEWPIE

PA PERKINS
POPEYE
SKIPPY (2 diff.)
WIMPY

NEWSPAPER: SATURDAY DAILY NEWS

Saturday Daily News. 1940's. 13/16" litho. BW & red. Lou Fox. 8 seen.

ABNER'S MA
APPLE MARY
DAN DUNN
DENNIE

ELLA CINDERS
JEFF
LI'L ABNER
MUTT

NEWSPAPERS: CONTEST SETS

Various Newspapers. 1930's. 1¼" cell. except as noted. Bastian and Offset Gravure. Serially numbered for daily drawings to win "Valuable Prizes." 94 seen.

BUFFALO EVENING NEWS. Blue & white with fleshtone faces. (9)

BEN WEBSTER
BUCK ROGERS (with mustache)
ELLA CINDERS
MUTT AND JEFF (pictures MUTT)
PAM

"POP"
REG'LAR FELLARS
SKEEZIX
SKY ROADS

DETROIT TIMES. 1" and 1¼" cell. Red & white with fleshtone faces. (9)

BARNEY GOOGLE*
DER CAPTAIN**
JIGGS*
KATZENJAMMER KIDS**
  *Seen only in 1" size.
**Seen only in 1¼" size.

SKIPPY
THE NEBBS*
TILLIE

JOHNSTOWN TRIBUNE. Blue & white with fleshtone faces. (3)

LITTLE ORPHAN ANNIE
MOON MULLINS (3/4 portrait)

REG'LAR FELLERS

LOS ANGELES EVENING EXPRESS. BW with fleshtone faces. (6)

BENNY
"CAP" STUBBS
JOE JINKS

LITTLE ORPHAN ANNIE
MOON MULLINS
PAM

MILWAUKEE SENTINEL. Blue & white with fleshtone faces. (6)

BOUND TO WIN
BRINGING UP FATHER
GUS AND GUSSIE

PETTING PATTY
THE NEBBS
TILLIE THE TOILER

NEWARK STAR-EAGLE. 1″ and 1¼″ cell. BW with fleshtone faces and numbers in black, red or blue. Both sizes show the newspaper name in black or red type. (13)

ETTA KETT
MINUTE MOVIES*
MR. BUNGLE
MUGGS McGINNIS
*Seen only in 1″ size.

NEBBS
S'MATTER POP
TAILSPIN TOMMY

NEW YORK EVENING JOURNAL. Red & white with fleshtone faces. (21)

ABIE
BING (full figure)
CASTOR OYL
DORA
DORA (full figure)
ELLA CINDERS
IGNATZ MOUSE
KRAZY KAT
KRAZY KAT (full figure)
LITTLE ANNIE ROONEY
LITTLE ANNIE ROONEY (full figure)

MUSH
MUSH (full figure)
PA PERKINS
PA PERKINS (full figure)
POPEYE
POPEYE (full figure)
RAINBOW DUFFY
ROD
THE VILLIAN
TIM TYLER (full figure)

NEW YORK SUNDAY AMERICAN. Red & white with fleshtone faces. (20)

ARCHIE
BARNEY GOOGLE
BOOB McNUTT
BUTTERCUP
CASPER
DER CAPTAIN
DER PROFESSOR
HAPPY HOOLIGAN
JIGGS
KATZENJAMMER KIDS

MAC
MAGGIE
MAMA KATZENJAMMER
MARGY
MAUD
ROSIE
SKIPPY
SPARK-PLUG
TILLIE
TOOTS

PITTSBURGH POST-GAZETTE. Blue & white with fleshtone faces. (7)

ANDY GUMP
BUCK ROGERS
HAROLD TEEN
MOON MULLINS (profile)

ORPHAN ANNIE
UNCLE WALT
WINNIE WINKLE

WESTERN THEATRE PREMIUM CO.

Numbered set of 50. SEE PAGE 29.

FLOWERS/FRUIT

FLOWERS

King Bee Tobacco and Cigarettes. Circa 1900. 7/8″ cell. MC. L.C. White. Filled backs. 14 seen.

BACHELOR'S BUTTON   HOPE IN LOVE
CHINA ASTER   I WILL THINK OF IT.
CHRYSANTHEMUM   I LOVE
DAHLIA   FOREVER THINE
GOLDEN ROD   ENCOURAGEMENT
HYACINTH   JEALOUSY
LILAC   FIRST EMOTION OF LOVE

LILY   PURITY
PEACH BLOSSOM   THIS HEART IS THINE
ROSE BUD MOSS   CONFESSION OF LOVE
SUNFLOWER   YOUR DEVOUT ADMIRER
TEAROSE   ALWAYS LOVELY
TULIP   DECLARATION OF LOVE
VIOLET   FAITHFULNESS

NOTE: Apparently there is a second set, mfr'd by W&H. 2 seen.

TULIP. SWEET CHARITY.

VIOLET. FAITHFULNESS.

FLOWERS & FRUIT

American Pepsin Gum. Circa 1900. 7/8″ cell. MC. W&H. 20 seen.

AMERICAN BEAUTY.
CHRYSANTHEMUM   SLIGHTED LOVE.
DAISYS AND BLACK EYES. INNOCENCE
   AND LOVE.
DELAWARE PEACH
EASTER LILY. PURITY.
FORGET-ME-NOT
FUCHSIA. TASTE.
GOLDEN ROD.
GOLDEN ROD. PRECAUTION.
LILAC. EMOTIONS OF LOVE

LILY OF THE VALLEY. UNCONSCIOUS
   SWEETNESS
MAPLE LEAF*
ORANGE BLOSSOMS. YOUR PURITY,
   EQUALS YOUR LOVLINESS
PANSEY. SWEET THOUGHTS.
PANSY.*
PINK CARNATION. WOMEN'S LOVE.
SCOTCH THISTLE
TUBE ROSE. DANGEROUS PLEASURES
TULIP. SWEET CHARITY.
VIOLET. FAITHFULNESS.

Color variety seen.

NOTE: PANSY has also been seen with backpaper of Country Club tobacco.

STATE FLOWERS

Issuer Unknown. 1930's. 13/16" litho. MC. Geraghty. **Set of 48.**

ALABAMA GOLDENROD
ARIZONA SAGUARO
ARKANSAS APPLE BLOSSOM
CALIFORNIA GOLDEN POPPY
COLORADO COLUMBINE
CONNECTICUT MOUNTAIN LAUREL
DELAWARE PEACH BLOSSOM
FLORIDA ORANGE BLOSSOM
GEORGIA CHEROKEE ROSE
IDAHO SYRINGA
ILLINOIS VIOLET
INDIANA ZINNIA
IOWA WILD ROSE
KANSAS SUN FLOWER
KENTUCKY GOLDENROD
LOUISIANA MAGNOLIA
MAINE PINE CONE and TASSEL
MARYLAND BLACK-EYED SUSAN
MASSACHUSETTS TRAILING ARBUTUS
MICHIGAN APPLE BLOSSOM
MINNESOTA MOCCASIN FLOWER
MISSISSIPPI MAGNOLIA
MISSOURI HAWTHORN
MONTANA BITTER ROOT

NEBRASKA GOLDENROD
NEVADA SAGEBRUSH
NEW HAMPSHIRE PURPLE LILAC
NEW JERSEY VIOLET
NEW MEXICO YUCCA
NEW YORK ROSE
NORTH CAROLINA OXEYE DAISY
NORTH DAKOTA WILD ROSE
OHIO SCARLET CARNATION
OKLAHOMA MISTLETOE
OREGON OREGON GRAPE
PENNSYLVANIA MOUNTAIN LAUREL
RHODE ISLAND VIOLET
SOUTH CAROLINA YELLOW JESSAMINE
SOUTH DAKOTA PASQUE FLOWER
TENNESSEE PASSION-FLOWER
TEXAS BLUE BONNET
UTAH SEGO LILY
VERMONT RED CLOVER
VIRGINIA AMERICAN DOGWOOD
WASHINGTON RHODODENDRON
WEST VIRGINIA RHODODENDRON
WISCONSIN VIOLET
WYOMING INDIAN PAINT BRUSH

FOOD

ICE CREAM

Good Humor Ice Cream. 1930's. 13/16'' cell., except as noted. Blue, orange & white. W&H. 12 seen.

CHIEF (1½'')
CAPTAIN (1¼'')
A.B.C. ALWAYS BE CAREFUL*
Always STOP at Curb
Cross at CORNERS*
CROSS Streets Cautiously*
I MUST BE CAREFUL*
PLAY on Sidewalks
PLAY SAFE and Play Tomorrow
Slow Down, Why Hurry?
STOP, LOOK, LISTEN
USE Your Eyes — Look!

*Also seen with A.B.C. SAFETY CLUB in place of Good Humor Safety Club.

GEOGRAPHICAL

FLAGS

Probably the most popular subject for early button sets was flags, and the varieties were exhaustive. Flags—national flags, state flags, city flags, historical flags, college pennants—appeared in a variety of sizes, in celluloid and lithographed on tin, with open backs and closed backs, in metal frames with a pin soldered on the back or with an easel back, as tabs, and die-cut from celluloid sheets. Most made a heroic effort to reproduce the colors of the original and to spell the sometimes exotic names correctly. Mfrs. included W&H, Bastian, Pulver, Green Duck, and even the City Button Works of NY. All the large users of buttons issued flag sets (Sweet Caporal, High Admiral, American Pepsin Gum), as did many others—Between the Acts and Duke Cigarettes, Weyman & Bros. Tobacco, Wrigley's Sweet 16 Gum, Wischmanns, Cameo Pepsin Gum, Earl Confections, Mac-Farlane Candy, Brunners and Wagner Bakeries, Sheffield Milk, Ware's Coffee, Nabisco Cereal. One enterprising manufacturer took the ultimate step and named his product Flagum.

No attempt has been made to catalog the many sets and endless varieties of flag buttons.

COATS OF ARMS

American Pepsin Gum. Circa 1900. 7/8" cell. MC. W&H. All have red lettering, but CHILI and CUBA have also been seen with black lettering. 12 seen.

CANADA	FRANCE.
CHILI.	GERMANY
CUBA	ITALY
ENGLAND	MEXICO
FRANCE	RUSSIA

STATE MAPS

American Pepsin Gum and **Adams Tutti Fruitti Gum.** Circa 1900. 7/8″ cell. BW & pink or yellow. W&H. **Apparently a set of 15.**

CALIFORNIA	IOWA	NEW JERSEY
CONNECTICUT	MAINE	NEW YORK
DELAWARE	MASSACHUSETTS	OHIO
ILLINOIS	MICHIGAN	PENNSYLVANIA
INDIANA	MISSOURI	VERMONT

STATE SEALS

American Pepsin Gum. Circa 1900. 7/8″ cell. MC. W&H. 9 seen.

ALASKA	ILLINOIS.	NEW YORK.
CALIFORNIA.	INDIANA.	OHIO.
DELAWARE*	INDIAN TERRITORY	PENNSYLVANIA.

*Cut-down print.

NOTE: These have been seen with state name in both black and red. Also, 1¼″ versions have been seen with Cameo Pepsin Gum backpaper for DISTRICT OF COLUMBIA, KANSAS and MICHIGAN; and with El Capitan Chewing Gum backpaper for INDIANA.

STATE SEALS

Sweet Caporal Cigarette. Circa 1900. 7/8″ cell. MC. W&H. 47 states (Oklahoma not issued) plus District of Columbia. State of Washington is a portrait of George Washington. **Set of 48.**

TRAVEL & ADVENTURE

Issuer Unknown. 1930's. 13/16" litho. MC. Bastian. Numbered on curl, although some numbers are almost impossible to read because of the poor printing. Also, Bastian identification is sometimes absent. **Numbered set of 30.**

1 GREAT BRITAIN
2 SPAIN
3 JAPAN
4 ITALY
5 BELGIUM
6
7 MEXICO
8
9 CAPTAIN KIDD
10 TRAVEL IN INDIA
11 TELL IT TO THE MARINES
12 TRAVEL IN JAPAN
13 TRAVEL IN NORWAY
14 TRAVEL IN EGYPT
15 FOREIGN LEGION

16 TRAVEL IN ITALY
17 TRAVEL IN THE ARCTIC
18 AMERICAN EAGLE
19 IN SPAIN
20 TRAVEL IN MEXICO
21 UNDER FULL SAIL
22 HELLO SAILOR
23 UNCLE SAM
24 CHIEF OF CHIEFS
25 KEEP SMILING
26 CUBA
27 RIDE M COWBOY
28 LION
29 ACE
30 SPIRIT OF '76

MILITARY

UNIFORMS

American Pepsin Gum. Circa 1900. 7/8" cell. MC. W&H. 6 seen.

CONTINENTAL*	OFFICER
PRIVATE	ZOUAVE (facing left)
MAJOR GENERAL	ZOUAVE (facing right)

Color variety seen.

AIR INSIGNIA, WW II

Kellogg's Pep. 1940's. 13/16" litho. MC. No mfr. Set of 36.

2D BOMBARDMENT SQUADRON
17TH BOMBARDMENT SQUADRON
25TH BOMBARDMENT SQUADRON
27TH FIGHTER SQUADRON
29TH BOMBARDMENT SQUADRON
34TH BOMBARDMENT SQUADRON
41ST BOMBARDMENT SQUADRON
44TH FIGHTER SQUADRON
48TH BOMBARDMENT SQUADRON
53RD BOMBARDMENT SQUADRON
56TH BOMBARDMENT SQUADRON
70TH BOMBARDMENT SQUADRON
94TH PURSUIT SQUADRON
96TH BOMBARDMENT SQUADRON
99TH BOMBARDMENT SQUADRON
103RD OBSERVATION SQUADRON
306TH BOMBARDMENT SQUADRON
370TH BOMBARDMENT SQUADRON
385TH BOMBARDMENT SQUADRON

391ST BOMBARDMENT SQUADRON
402ND BOMBARDMENT SQUADRON
424TH BOMBARDMENT SQUADRON
431ST BOMBARDMENT SQUADRON
471ST BOMBARDMENT SQUADRON
MARINE BOMBING SQUAD 433
MARINE FIGHTER SQUADRON VMF-224
MARINE TORPEDO BOMBING-232
NAVY BOMBING-FIGHTING
  SQUADRON-12
NAVY BOMBING SQUADRON-11
NAVY CRUISER-SCOUTING
  SQUADRON-2
NAVY PATROL SQUADRON-23
NAVY STAGRON-14
NAVY TORPEDO SQUADRON-3
NAVY TORPEDO SQUADRON-32
VB-13
VO-3

NOTE: This 13/16" Kellogg's Pep litho inscribed 98TH DIVISION, an Army unit, is apparently part of another set. The lettering on the reverse is red rather than blue.

MOVIES

THE SECRET 4

Issuer Unknown. 1940. 7/8″ cell. Red & white. W&H and Bastian. 10 seen.

EXALTED GOBEY
GRAND CYCLOPS
GREAT GOBLIN
IMPERIAL IMP
OMNIPOTENT OMP

REGAL RINGO
ROYAL KIZZARO
SUBLIME NABOB
SUPERIOR SULTAN
SUPREME WIZ

WITH STANLEY IN AFRICA

Issuer Unknown. 1922. 1¼″ cell. Blue & white. Bastian. 10 seen.

THE ADDAX
THE CAPE BUFFALO
THE ELAND
THE GUIB
THE HYDRAX
THE KLIPSPRINGER

THE MANDRILL
THE QUAGGA
THE WILDEBEEST
"WITH STANLEY IN AFRICA"
  (outline of Africa)

THE WIZARD OF OZ

Issuer Unknown. 1939. 7/8″ and 1¼″ cell. Orange, blue & white. Economy Novelty Co. The 7/8″ give the title in Spanish (EL MAGO DE OZ); the 1¼″ are numbered serially with the title in English. Each character appears in both sizes. 11 seen.

RAY BOLGER
JUDY GARLAND
JACK HALEY

BERT LAHR*
FRANK MORGAN

*Also seen in 7/8″ with the title EL BRUJO DE OZ.

25

MOVIE MONSTERS

Universal Pictures Co. Inc. 1960's. 7/8" litho. BW & one color. Elwar Ltd. **Set of 6.**

DRACULA
FRANKENSTEIN
THE CREATURE

THE MUMMY
THE PHANTOM
WOLF MAN

MOVIE STARS

Pender Breads (Norfolk, Va.). 1930's. 1" cell. BW pictures with name and two stars in red on white rim. Bastian. **Set of 11** listed on backpaper. (Also seen with just Bastian paper.)

LIONEL BARRYMORE
WALLACE BEERY
GARY COOPER
JOAN CRAWFORD
MARLENE DIETRICH
MARIE DRESSLER

KAY FRANCIS
CLARK GABLE
GRETA GARBO
ROBERT MONTGOMERY
NORMA SHEARER

MOVIE STARS

Quaker Puffed Wheat & Rice. 1948. 13/16" litho. BW, red & flesh. No mfr. **Set of 20.**

WILLIAM BENDIX A PARAMOUNT STAR
MACDONALD CAREY A PARAMOUNT STAR
JACK CARSON A WARNER BROS. STAR
JOAN CAULFIELD A PARAMOUNT STAR
WILLIAM DEMAREST A PARAMOUNT STAR
BILLY DEWOLFE A PARAMOUNT STAR
BILL ELLIOTT A REPUBLIC STAR
MONTE HALE A REPUBLIC STAR
WILLIAM HOLDEN A PARAMOUNT STAR
TIM HOLT AN RKO STAR

BETTY HUTTON A PARAMOUNT STAR
ALAN LADD A PARAMOUNT STAR
VERONICA LAKE A PARAMOUNT STAR
GUY MADISON A SELZNICK STAR
RAY MILLAND A PARAMOUNT STAR
ROBERT MITCHUM A SELZNICK-RKO STAR
DENNIS MORGAN A WARNER BROS. STAR
RONALD REAGAN A WARNER BROS. STAR
GAIL RUSSELL A PARAMOUNT STAR
LIZABETH SCOTT A PARAMOUNT STAR

MOVIE STARS

Quaker Puffed Wheat & Rice Sparkies. 1940's. 13/16"
litho. BW, red, yellow & flesh. No mfr. Similar to Quaker
Puffed Wheat & Rice set but line drawings rather than
photos. All are PARAMOUNT STARS. 11 seen.

WILLIAM BENDIX
JOAN CAULFIELD
WILLIAM DEMAREST
WILLIAM HOLDEN
BETTY HUTTON
DOROTHY LAMOUR

RAY MILLAND
ROBERT PRESTON
LIZABETH SCOTT
RANDOLPH SCOTT
SONNY TUFTS

MOVIE STARS

"Sampeck" Triple-Service Suit. 1920's. 1¼" cell. BW.
"Bim" the Button & Badge Man. Stars not identified.
4 seen.

Fatty Arbuckle
Charlie Chaplin

Douglas Fairbanks
William S. Hart

MOVIE STARS

Sandyval Graphics Ltd. Personality Buttons.
1960's. 1¾" cell. BW. No mfr. Stars not identified. Figures in parentheses indicate the number
of different portraits of that star. **Set of 84.**

FATTY ARBUCKLE & BUSTER KEATON
FRED ASTAIRE
ASTAIRE & GINGER ROGERS
THEDA BARA
JOHN BARRYMORE
WALLACE BEERY
HUMPHREY BOGART
BOGART & BETTY DAVIS
BOGART & KATHERINE HEPBURN
RAY BOLGER

MARLON BRANDO
JOE E. BROWN & GINGER ROGERS
YUL BRYNNER
LON CHANEY
CHARLIE CHAPLIN (6)
GARY COOPER
COOPER & INGRID BERGMAN
JACKIE COOPER
JOAN CRAWFORD
BETTE DAVIS (2)

JAMES DEAN	HAROLD LLOYD (2)
MARLENE DIETRICH (3)	CAROLE LOMBARD
W.C. FIELDS (4)	SOPHIA LOREN
ERROL FLYNN	PETER LORRE
CLARK GABLE (3)	BELA LUGOSI (& DINNER)
GRETA GARBO (2)	FREDERIC MARCH as Dr. Jekyll
JOHN GARFIELD	MARX BROTHERS
JUDY GARLAND	GROUCHO MARX (2)
CARY GRANT	VICTOR McLAGLEN
JACK HALEY	MARILYN MONROE (3)
JEAN HARLOW (2)	LAURENCE OLIVIER
WILLIAM S. HART	BILL "BOJANGLES" ROBINSON
RITA HAYWORTH (2)	EDWARD G. ROBINSON
KATHERINE HEPBURN	MICKEY ROONEY & JUDY GARLAND
LESLIE HOWARD & NORMA SHEARER	SHIRLEY TEMPLE
BORIS KARLOFF & ELSA LANCHESTER	RUDOLPH VALENTINO (2)
BUSTER KEATON	ERICH VON STROHEIM
GENE KELLY	JOHN WAYNE (2)
KING KONG	MAE WEST & GEORGE RAFT
BERT LAHR	Slide: IF ANNOYED WHEN HERE PLEASE
CHARLES LAUGHTON	TELL THE MANAGEMENT
LAUREL & HARDY	

MOVIE STARS

Western Theatre Premium Co. 1930's. 13/16" litho. Blue & white. Geraghty. Issued with both Geraghty and Western Theatre identification on reverse. 9 seen.

JOE E. BROWN	JANET GAYNOR	HAROLD LLOYD
NANCY CARROLL	LEON JANNEY	VICTOR McLAGLEN
GARY COOPER	LAUREL & HARDY	WHEELER & WOOLSEY

MOVIE STARS

Western Theatre Premium Co. 1930's. 13/16'' and 7/8'' litho. The 13/16'' set is BW & red; the 7/8'' set is both BW & red and BW, red & yellow. No mfr. Appears in the 7/8'' size with either a Chicago or a Los Angeles address on the curl, and in both sizes without any issuer identification. The numbered characters are the same in all three sets, but design variations occur. **Numbered set of 50.**

1 WALTER LANTZ BILL NOLAN'S OSWALD the lucky RABBIT
2 WALTER LANTZ BILL NOLAN'S Oswald's KITTY
3 LOONEY TUNES BOSKO
4 LOONEY TUNES LITTLE WILBUR
5 LOONEY TUNES BOSKO'S DOG BRUNO
6 MERRIE MELODIES GOOPY
7 LOONEY TUNES HONEY
8 TERRY-TOONS (unnamed character)
9 TERRY-TOONS (unnamed character)
10 TERRY-TOONS (unnamed character)
11 TERRY-TOONS FARMER ALFALFA
12 CHARLES MINTZ'S YIPPY COLUMBIA PICTURES
13 CHARLES MINTZ'S KITTY KAT COLUMBIA PICTURES
14 CHARLES MINTZ'S KRAZY KAT COLUMBIA PICTURES
15 CHARLES MINTZ'S VONTZY COLUMBIA PICTURES
16 CHARLES MINTZ'S SCRAPPY COLUMBIA PICTURES
17 MARTY MONK CARTOONS B. LaVero 1931
18 AESOP'S FABLES MIKE
19 AESOP'S FABLES DON
20 AESOP'S FABLES JUDGE
21 AESOP'S FABLES AL
22 AESOP'S FABLES WAFFLES
23 AESOP'S FABLES COUNTESS
24 AESOP'S FABLES PUFFIE
25 KO-KO MAX FLEISHER'S TALKATOONS
26 BIMBO MAX FLEISHER'S TALKATOONS
27 BETTY BOOP MAX FLEISHER'S TALKATOONS
28 JIMMIE by SWINNERTON "LITTLE JIMMIE"
29 BOOB McNUTT by "RUBE" Goldberg
30 CASPER "TOOTS & CASPER" by JIMMY MURPHY
31 "BARNEY GOOGLE" DEBECK
32 TILLIE TILLIE THE TOILER BY RUSS WESTOVER
33 MAC TILLIE THE TOILER BY RUSS WESTOVER
34 "THE KATZENJAMMER KIDS" HANS & FRITZ by KNERR
35 JIGGS "BRINGING UP FATHER" by GEO. McMANUS
36 MAGGIE "BRINGING UP FATHER" by GEO. McMANUS
37 POPEYE "THIMBLE THEATRE" by SEGAR
38 WALT GASOLINE ALLEY By King
39 ELLA "ELLA CINDERS" by BILL CONSELMAN & CHARLEY PLUMB
40 HAROLD "HAROLD TEEN" by CARL ED

41 "MOON MULLINS" MOON by WILLARD
42 PA "POLLY AND HER PALS" by CLIFF STERRETT
43 ANDY GUMP THE GUMPS by SIDNEY SMITH
44 CHESTER THE GUMPS by SIDNEY SMITH
45 OLD DOC YAC DOC
46 JOE MR. AND MRS by BRIGGS
47 PA "WINNIE WINKLE" by BRANNER
48 BLACKIE "ELLA CINDERS" by BILL CONSELMAN & CHARLIE PLUM
49 PERRY "WINNIE WINKLE" by BRANNER
50 SKEEZIX GASOLINE ALLEY by KING

NOTE: Number 46 has also been seen as a 13/16" tab with BUY Chase's CANDIES on the back.

MOVIE STARS

W & S Theatre Premium Co. 1930's. 13/16" litho. Blue & white. No mfr. 9 seen.

NANCY CARROL	LUCKY LINDY	MICKEY MOUSE
CHARLES CHAPLIN	HAROLD LLOYD	MARY PICKFORD
HOOT GIBSON	KEN MAYNARD	CHAS. (BUDDY) ROGERS

MOVIE STARS

Issuer Unknown. 1930's. 13/16'' litho. Blue, white, yellow & flesh. No mfr. **Set of 25.**

RICHARD ARLEN
GEORGE BANCROFT
WARNER BAXTER
CONSTANCE BENNETT
JOAN BENNETT
CLAUDETTE COLBERT
RONALD COLMAN
JACKIE COOPER
MARION DAVIES
MARLENE DIETRICH
RICHARD DIX
MARIE DRESSLER
SALLEY EILERS

CHARLES FARRELL
CLARK GABLE
GRETA GARBO
JANET GAYNOR
HELEN HAYES
BUSTER KEATON
FREDERICK MARCH
TOM MIX & TONY
ROBERT MONTGOMERY
RAMON NOVARRO
WILL ROGERS
NORMA SHEARER

CAUTION: Inks used to print this series are water-soluble—buttons cannot be cleaned without risk of losing picture.

MOVIE STARS

Issuer Unknown. 1930's. 13/16'' litho. This listing may comprise several distinct sets: red & white vs. blue & white; Greenduck vs. no mfr.; and different treatment of the portraits—head alone vs. head and torso. For now, all are listed here. 16 seen, plus color varieties.

JOE. E. BROWN
NANCY CARROLL (2 diff.)
GARY COOPER (2 diff.)
DOUGLAS FAIRBANKS JR.
HOOT GIBSON
LEON JANNEY
HAROLD LLOYD (2 diff.)

KEN MAYNARD
VICTOR McLAGLEN
JACK OAKIE
GEORGE O'BRIEN
MARY PICKFORD
CHARLES (BUDDY) ROGERS

MOVIE STARS

Issuer Unknown. 1930's. 7/8'' cell. BW or light brown. No mfr. 30 seen.

RENEE ADOREE   Metro-Goldwyn Mayer
MONTE BLUE   A Warner Bros. Star
JOAN CRAWFORD   Metro-Goldwyn Mayer
KARL DANE   Metro-Goldwyn Mayer
ROY D'ARCY   Metro-Goldwyn Mayer
REGINALD DENNY   Universal Star
BILLIE DOVE   Universal Star
LOUISE FAZENDA   A Warner Bros. Star
HOOT GIBSON   Universal Star
WILLIAM HANES   Metro-Goldwyn Mayer
JEAN HERSHOT   Universal Star
FRED HUMES   Universal Western Star
RAYMOND KEANE   Universal Star
NORMAN KERRY   Universal Star
ARTHUR LANE   Universal Star

LAURA LA PLANTE   Universal Star
GEORGE LEWIS   Universal Star
TIM McCOY   Metro-Goldwyn Mayer
JOE MURPHY
JAMES MURRY   Metro-Goldwyn Mayer
MARION NIXON   Universal Star
JACK PERRIN   Universal Western Star
MARY PHILBIN   Universal Star
EDDIE PHILLIPS   Universal Star
CHARLES RAY   Universal Star
RIN-TIN-TIN   A Warner Bros. Star*
DOROTHY SEBASTIAN   Metro-Goldwyn Mayer
GLENN TRYON   Universal Star
AL WILSON   Universal Star
BARBARA WORTH   Universal Star

Also seen with Phila. Badge backpaper.

MOVIE STARS

Issuer Unknown. 1930's. 15/16'' litho. BW & flesh. Greenduck. Numbered. 12 seen.

2 FRED ASTAIRE
3 GRETA GARBO
8 MYRNA LOY
10 NORMA SHEARER
14 SPENCER TRACY
15 JOAN BLONDELL

17 FREDDIE BARTHOLOMEW
18 CLAUDETTE COLBERT
20 EDWARD G. ROBINSON
21 ALICE FAYE
22 JANE WITHERS
23 DON AMECHE

MUSIC

THE BEATLES

Seltaeb. 1964. 7/8″ litho. BW & red, orange, or blue. Green Duck. 9 seen, plus color varieties.

I LOVE THE BEATLES!
I'M A BEATLE BUG
I'M A BEATLES BOOSTER (long hair)
I'M 4 BEATLES
MEMBER BEATLES FAN CLUB

THE BEATLES   GEORGE HARRISON
   (photo)
THE BEATLES   JOHN LENNON (photo)
THE BEATLES   PAUL McCARTNEY (photo)
THE BEATLES   RINGO "RINGS" STARR
   (photo)

ELVIS PRESLEY

E.P.E. (Elvis Presley Enterprises) 1956. 7/8″ litho. MC, mostly RWB. Green Duck. 10 seen, plus color varieties.

PICTURE OF ELVIS (4)
   ALWAYS YOURS ELVIS
   ELVIS PRESLEY
   ELVIS PRESLEY (guitar & notes)
   I LIKE ELVIS

RECORDS (4)
   "DON'T BE CRUEL" (broken heart)
   "LOVE ME TENDER" (Elvis)
   "SHAKE-RATTLE AND ROLL" (dice)
   "YOU'RE NOTHIN' BUT A HOUN'
      DOG" (dog)

SLOGANS (2)
   ELVIS
   I LIKE ELVIS

ELVIS PRESLEY GOLD RECORDS

Issuer Unknown. Circa 1956. 7/8″ litho. BW & gold. No mfr. Made to look like a gold record with Elvis' picture in the center. 7 seen.

ANY WAY YOU WANT ME
BLUE SUEDE SHOES
DON'T BE CRUEL
HEARTBREAK HOTEL

HOUND DOG
I WANT YOU, I NEED YOU, I LOVE YOU
LOVE ME TENDER

GOLD RECORDS

Issuer Unknown. Circa 1956. 7/8" litho. Various colors and gold. No mfr. MADE IN U.S.A. on curl. Made to look like a gold record with drawing in the center. 12 seen.

AIN'T THAT A SHAME (broken heart)
BLUE SUEDE SHOES (shoes)
GREEN DOOR (door)
HEARTBREAK HOTEL (canopy)
HOUND DOG (dog)
I WANT NEED LOVE U (heart)

LOVE ME TENDER (guitarist)
MY PRAYER (praying hands)
ROCK AROUND THE CLOCK (clock)
ROCK N ROLL (dancers)
SINGING THE BLUES (notes)
YOU'LL NEVER KNOW (question mark)

PURPLE PEOPLE EATER

Issuer Unknown. 1958. 13/16" litho. Purple & white. Green Duck. 3 seen.

I AM A PURPLE PEOPLE EATER (monster)
I'M A PURPLE PEOPLE EATER (music notes)

PURPLE PEOPLE EATER (monster)

COMPOSERS

Griffith Music Foundation. 1930's. 1" cell. BW & one color. No mfr. Composers not identified. 3 seen.

CESAR FRANCK   TCHAIKOVSKY   RICHARD WAGNER

RECORDING STARS

Issuer Unknown. 1950's. 7/8" litho. BW or brown picture on single-color background. Green Duck. Reverse says "A MERCURY RECORDS/DECCA/COLUMBIA RECORDS RECORDING STAR"—identified in parentheses below. 8 seen.

DAVID CARROLL (Mercury)
RUSTY DRAPER (Mercury)
BILL HALEY FAN (Decca)
FRANKIE LAINE (Columbia)

JOY LAYNE (Mercury)
RALPH MARTERIE (Mercury)
NICK NOBLE (Mercury)
SARAH VAUGHAN (Mercury)

ORGANIZATIONS

ORGANIZATIONS

American Pepsin Gum. Circa 1900. 7/8" cell. MC. W&H. Primarily fraternal orders and religious or service groups, each showing the organizational insignia. Some show only the insignia without the name. 40 seen.

AMERICAN FIREMEN.
ANCIENT ORDER OF FORESTERS OF AMERICA F. OF A.
ANCIENT ORDER OF HIBERNIANS
A.O.U.W. (insignia only)
BAPTIST YOUNG PEOPLE'S UNION
BROTHERHOOD OF RAIL ROAD TRAINMEN
CATHOLIC BENEVOLENT LEGION
CATHOLIC MUTUAL BENEFIT ASS'N.
CATHOLIC MUTUAL BENEFJT ASS'N. (insignia only)
ELKS B.P.O.E
ELKS B.P.O.E (insignia only)
EPWORTH LEAGUE. LOOK UP LIFT UP
GOOD TEMPLARS
GRAND ARMY OF THE REPUBLIC
IMPROVED ORDER OF RED MEN (hatchet)
IMPROVED ORDER OF RED MEN (Indian head)
INDEPENDENT ORDER OF FORESTERS
INDEPENDENT ORDER OF FORESTERS (insignia only)
INDEPENDENT ORDER OF ODD FELLOWS.

JR. ORDER UNITED AMERICAN MECHANICS
JR. ORDER UNITED AMERICAN MECHANICS (insignia only)
KNIGHTS OF HONOR
KNIGHTS OF PYTHIAS
KNIGHTS OF THE GOLDEN EAGLE
KNIGHTS OF THE GOLDEN EAGLE (insignia only)
KNIGHTS OF THE MACCABEES
KNIGHTS TEMPLAR
LOYAL ORANGE INSTITUTION.
MASONIC
MASONIC (insignia only)
MODERN WOODMEN OF AMERICA
MYSTIC CHAIN
MYSTIC SHRINE
ORDER UNITED AMERICAN MECHANICS
PAROCHIAL SCHOOL
PATRIOTIC ORDER SONS OF AMERICA
PATRONS OF HUSBANDRY
ROYAL ARCANUM
ST. PATRICK'S ALLIANCE
WOODMEN OF THE WORLD

UNIONS

Peters Brotherhood Overalls. 1900's. 7/8" cell. MC. W&H. 6 seen.

B of L E (Brotherhood of Locomotive Engineers)
B of L E (different insignia)
B of L F (Brotherhood of Locomotive Firemen)
B of L F and E (Brotherhood of Locomotive Firemen and Engineers)
B.R.T. (Brotherhood of Railroad Trainmen)
O.R.C. (Order of Railway Conductors of America)

UNIONS

Sweet-Orr Overalls and Pants. 1900's. 7/8" cell. Various colors. W&H. 17 seen.

B of L E (Brotherhood of Locomotive Engineers)
B of L F (Brotherhood of Locomotive Firemen)
B of R.T. of A (Brotherhood of Railroad Trainmen of America)
B R R T (Brotherhood of Railroad Trainmen)
BROTHERHOOD OF PAINTERS & DECORATORS OF AMERICA
CARPENTERS' UNION
CIGAR MAKERS INTERNATIONAL UNION OF AMERICA
I.A.A.M.
IAB & SIW of A (International Association of Bridge & Structural Iron Workers of America)
I A of M INTERNATIONAL ASSOCIATION OF MACHINISTS
INTERNATIONAL ASSOCIATION OF MACHINISTS
NATIONAL ASSOCIATION OF STATIONARY ENGINEERS
SUNA (Switchmen's Union of North America)
TEAMSTERS UNION
U.M.W. of A. (United Mine Workers of America)
(insignia) (Bricklayers & Masons International Union)
(insignia) (unidentified)

NOTE: B of L E, B of L F and SUNA have also been seen in 3/4".

PERSONALITIES

CELEBRITIES

Personality Posters. 1960's. 1¾'' cell. BW. No mfr. Characters not identified. 35 seen.

MUHAMMAD ALI
WOODY ALLEN
THEDA BARA
BRIGITTE BARDOT
HARRY BELAFONTE
JEAN-PAUL BELMONDO
HUMPHREY BOGART
MARLON BRANDO
JAMES CAGNEY as Lon
   Chaney

MICHAEL CAINE
STOKELY CARMICHAEL
LON CHANEY, JR. as
   Wolfman
CHARLIE CHAPLIN
BILL COSBY
SALVADOR DALI
JAMES DEAN
BOB DYLAN
ALBERT EINSTEIN
W.C. FIELDS
PETER FONDA
ALLEN GINSBERG

ERNEST HEMINGWAY
TIMOTHY LEARY
SOPHIA LOREN
DAVID McCALLUM
MARILYN MONROE
NAPOLEON
PAUL NEWMAN
ADAM CLAYTON POWELL
ALAN ROSSI
BERTRAND RUSSELL
FRANK SINATRA
BARBRA STREISAND
RUDOLPH VALENTINO
ANDY WARHOL

DAVID LEVINE DRAWINGS

New York Review. 1966. 1¾'' and 6'' cell. No mfr. Numbered and identified on curl, except as noted. 20 seen.

A1. Johnson (showing scar)
A2. Pushkin
A3. Johnson (weeping crocodiles)
A4. Freud
A5. De Gaulle
A6. Einstein
A7. Ky
A8. Mao
A9. Bobby Kennedy*

A10. Picasso
A11. Johnson (in toga)
A12. Pope John
A13. Crocodile (weeping Johnsons)
A14. Beatles
A15. Johnson (as wolf)
A16. Keats
A17. Nietzche

Unnumbered
  Eisenhower
  Bertrand Russell

Also seen without data on curl.

NATIONAL HEROES

American Pepsin Gum. Circa 1900. 7/8" cell. BW & fleshtone. W&H. Athletes, celebrities, military leaders, poets, rulers, statesmen. Also seen with W&H paper. 84 seen.

ABBAS II KHEDIVE OF EGYPT
MARY ANDERSON.
EDDIE BALD CYCLIST, CHAMPION 1896.
P.T. BARNUM
HENRY WARD BEECHER.
SARA BERNHARDT
KARL OTTO VON BISMARCK
JAMES G. BLAINE
NAPOLEON BONAPARTE
EDWIN BOOTH.
GEN. WILLIAM BOOTH.
WILLIAM CULLEN BRYANT.
ROBERT BURNS
BUTLER, CYCLIST.*
GEN. BENJAMIN F. BUTLER
COL. WILLIAM F. CODY,
   BUFFALO BILL
THOMAS COOPER, CYCLIST.
CORBETT
GEN. G.A. CUSTER
WALTER DAMROSCH
JEFFERSON DAVIS.
CHAUNCEY DEPEW
CHARLES DICKENS
FRED DOUGLASS
THOS. A. EDISON
WILLIAM M. EVARTS
FITZSIMMONS
HON. J.B. FORAKER.
BENJAMIN FRANKLIN.
BENJAMIN FRANKLYN.
MAJ. GEN. JOHN C. FREMONT
GAUDAUR OARSMAN
Wm. E. GLADSTONE.
JAY GOULD.
GEN. ULYSSES S. GRANT.
HORACE GREELEY
NATHANIEL GREEN.
GEN. WINFIELD T. HANCOCK.
HANLAN OARSMAN
M.A. HANNA
PATRICK HENRY.
ROBERT G. INGERSOLL.

GEN. S. J. JACKSON, STONEWALL
   JACKSON
JOSEPH JEFFERSON
JOHNSON, CYCLIST.
LAFAYETTE.
GEN. ROBERT E. LEE
POPE LEO XIII.
JENNY LIND.
GEN. JOHN A. LOGAN
HENRY W. LONGFELLOW
MAJ. GEN. GEO. B. McCLELLAN
MAJ. GEN. GEORGE G. MEADE.
GEN. NELSON A . MILES.
SAM. F.B. MORSE.
HON. LEVI P. MORTON.
MULDOON WRESTLER
PADEREWSKI
REV. C.H. PARKHURST
ADELINA PATTI
HON. THOMAS C. PLATT.
MATTHEW STANLEY QUAY.
THOMAS B. REED.
LILLIAN RUSSEL
SANDOW.
SANGER, CYCLIST.
WALTER SCOTT
WILLIAM SHAKESPEARE
GEN. PHILIP H. SHERIDAN
JOHN SHERMAN.
GEN. WILLIAM T. SHERMAN.
JOHN L. SULLIVAN.
REV. T. DE WITT TALMAGE
ALFRED TENNYSON
ELLEN TERRY
F.T. TITUS, CYCLIST.
CORNELIUS VANDERBILT.
WILLIAM H. VANDERBILT.
QUEEN VICTORIA.
PRINCE OF WALES
DANIEL WEBSTER.
JOHN G. WHITTIER
WILLIAM II EMPEROR OF GERMANY
A.A. ZIMMERMAN, CHAMPION CYCLIST.

Also seen in tin frame, 15/16", long shank pin, with no issuer identification.

NATIONAL HEROES

American Pepsin Gum. Circa 1900. 7/8″ cell. MC. W&H. Athletes, celebrities, military leaders, poets, rulers, statesmen. 48 seen.

ALFONSO XIII. KING OF SPAIN.
BARRETT, CELEBRATED ENGLISH JOCKEY.
BERGEN, CELEBRATED AMERICAN JOCKEY.
PRINCE BISMARK, GERMAN STATESMAN.
NAPOLEON BONAPARTE, FRENCH GENERAL.
WILLIAM CULLEN BRYANT, AMERICAN POET.
ROBERT BURNS, SCOTCH POET.
LORD BYRON, ENGLISH POET.
JULIUS CAESAR, ROMAN GENERAL.
CARLOS I. KING OF PORTUGAL.
CHRISTIAN IX. KING OF DENMARK.
OLIVER CROMWELL, ENGLISH GENERAL.
CHARLES DICKENS, ENGLISH AUTHOR.
DOGGETT, CELEBRATED AMERICAN JOCKEY.
ADMIRAL FARRAGUT, AMERICAN NAVAL OFFICER.
PRESIDENT FAURE OF FRANCE.
ROBT. FITZSIMMONS, CHAMPION FIGHTER OF THE WORLD.
GEORGIOS I KING OF GREECE.
W.E. GLADSTONE, ENGLISH STATESMAN.
U.S. GRANT, AMERICAN GENERAL.
HAMILTON, CELEBRATED AMERICAN JOCKEY.
FRANZ JOSEF I EMPEROR OF AUSTRIA.
LEOPOLD II KING OF BELGIUM.
LI HUNG CHANG, CHINESE STATESMAN.

ABRAHAM LINCOLN, AMERICAN WAR PRESIDENT.
LOATES, CELEBRATED ENGLISH JOCKEY.
HENRY W. LONGFELLOW, AMERICAN POET.
QUEEN LOUISE OF PRUSSIA.
JOHN MILTON, ENGLISH POET.
ADMIRAL NELSON, ENGLISH NAVAL OFFICER.
NICHOLAS II CZAR OF RUSSIA.
OSBORNE CELEBRATED ENGLISH JOCKEY.
OSCAR II KING OF SWEDEN.
WM. SHAKESPEARE, ENGLISH POET.
PHIL SHERIDAN, AMERICAN GENERAL.
WM. T. SHERMAN, AMERICAN GENERAL.
SIMS, CELEBRATED AMERICAN JOCKEY.
TARAL CELEBRATED AMERICAN JOCKEY.
ALFRED TENNYSON, ENGLISH POET.
VICTORIA QUEEN OF ENGLAND.
GEN'L. VON MOLTKE, GERMAN GENERAL.
PRINCE OF WALES.
GEORGE WASHINGTON, AMERICAN GENERAL.
WEBB, CELEBRATED ENGLISH JOCKEY.
DUKE OF WELLINGTON, ENGLISH GENERAL.
JOHN. G. WHITTIER, AMERICAN POET.
WILHELM II EMPEROR OF GERMANY.
WILHELMINA QUEEN OF HOLLAND.

NOTE: The following have also been seen as 1¼″ cell. without issuer identification: BRYANT, BURNS, DICKENS, LONGFELLOW, QUEEN LOUISE, TENNYSON, WHITTIER.

NATIONAL HEROES

Yank Junior (Clothing). 1934. 13/16" litho. MC. Geraghty? **Set of 16.**

ABRAHAM LINCOLN
ADMIRAL GEORGE DEWEY
BENJAMIN FRANKLIN
"BUFFALO BILL" CODY
CHIEF SITTING BULL*
COLONEL THEODORE ROOSEVELT
COMMODORE OLIVER A. PERRY*
DANIEL BOONE

GENERAL GEORGE CUSTER
GENERAL GEORGE WASHINGTON
GENERAL ROBERT E. LEE
GENERAL ULYSSES S. GRANT
JOHN PAUL JONES
"KIT" CARSON
NATHAN HALE
PAUL REVERE*

*Also seen with Geraghty logo in place of Yank Junior identification. Others in series give no mfr.

PRESIDENTS

AMERICAN PEPSIN GUM

American Pepsin Gum. Circa 1900. 7/8" cell. BW. W&H. Portrait, name and years in office. Washington to McKinley. **Set of 24.**

RKO

RKO. Issued between 1929 and 1932. 1¼" cell. MC. Bastian. Portrait, name and years in office. Washington to Hoover. (Also issued without the RKO identification.) **Set of 30.**

ISSUER UNKNOWN

Issuer Unknown. 1900's. 7/8" cell. MC with gold background. Bastian. Portrait and name. Only the following 9 have been seen: Arthur; Garfield; Grant; (B) Harrison; Hayes; Jefferson; Lincoln; McKinley; and (T) Roosevelt.

ISSUER UNKNOWN

Issuer Unknown. Circa 1930. 13/16" litho. Blue, white, yellow & flesh. No mfr. Portrait and name. Washington to Hoover (William H. Taft also incorrectly issued as Howard H. Taft). **Set of 31** including the error.

CAUTION: Inks used to print this series are water-soluble—buttons cannot be cleaned without risk of losing picture.

ISSUER UNKNOWN

Issuer Unknown. Issued between 1945 and 1952. 13/16" litho. RWB with stars and stripes border. No mfr. Portrait, name and years in office. Washington to Truman. **Set of 32.**

SHIPS

AMERICA'S CUP WINNERS

American Pepsin Gum. Circa 1900. 7/8" cell. MC but mainly blue & green. W&H. Each of these was issued in two varieties: one with blue skies, the other with white skies. Some of the latter have red pennants. 10 seen.

DEFENDER 1895
MAYFLOWER 1886
PURITAN 1885

VIGILANT 1893
VOLUNTEER 1887

OCEAN LINERS

American Pepsin Gum. Circa 1900. 7/8" cell. MC but mainly blue & green. W&H. 17 seen.

AMERICAN LINE STEAMSHIP
  NEW YORK
  PARIS
  PARIS.
  ST. LOUIS.
  ST. PAUL.
ANCHOR LINE STEAMSHIP
  CITY OF ROME.
CUNARD LINE
  ETRURIA
  SERVIA
  UMBRIA
CUNARD LINE STEAMSHIP
  CAMPANIA.

FRENCH LINE
  LA NORMANDIE
FRENCH LINE STEAMSHIP
  LA BRETAGNE.
HAMBURG AMERICAN LINE
  NORMANNIA.
NORTH GERMAN LLOYD
  ELBE.
WHITE STAR LINE
  BRITANNIC
  MAJESTIC
  TEUTONIC

UNITED STATES WAR SHIPS

American Pepsin Gum. Circa 1900. 7/8'' cell. MC but mainly blue & green. W&H. This series is virtually identical to the WHITE SQUADRON series below, except that these have blue skies and W.S. have white skies. Also, W.S. ships have RWB flags, these do not. 17 seen.

UNITED STATES WAR SHIP
  ATLANTA
  BALTIMORE
  BOSTON
  CHICAGO.
  CONCORD
  CUSHING.
  DOLPHIN.
  MIANTONOMAH
  MINNEAPOLIS.

NEWARK
NEW-YORK.
PETREL
PHILADELPHIA
VESUVIUS
YORKTOWN

U.S. CRUISER
  CHARLESTON
  S. FRANCISCO

THE WHITE SQUADRON

American Pepsin Gum. Circa 1900. 7/8'' cell. MC but mainly blue & green. W&H. 18 seen.

UNITED STATES WAR SHIP
  ATLANTA
  BALTIMORE.
  BOSTON
  CHICAGO
  CONCORD
  CUSHING.
  DOLPHIN.
  MIANTONOMAH
  MINNEAPOLIS.

NEWARK
NEW YORK.
NEW-YORK.
PETREL
PHILADELPHIA
VESUVIUS
YORKTOWN

U.S CRUISER
  CHARLESTON
  S. FRANCISCO

MISCELLANEOUS

American Pepsin Gum. Circa 1900. 7/8'' cell. MC but mainly blue & green. W&H. 2 seen.

GREAT EASTERN

STEAM YACHT

43

SPANISH-AMERICAN WARSHIPS

Issuer Unknown. Circa 1898. 1¼" cell. MC. W&H. 35 seen.

U.S. BATTLESHIP (9)
  ALABAMA
  INDIANA
  IOWA
  KEARSAGE
  KENTUCKY
  MASSACHUSETTS
  OREGON
  TEXAS
  WISCONSIN

U.S. CRUISER (16)
  BALTIMORE
  BANCROFT
  BOSTON
  BROOKLYN

  CHARLESTON
  CINCINNATI
  COLUMBIA
  MARBLEHEAD
  MINNEAPOLIS
  MONTGOMERY
  NEWARK
  NEW ORLEANS
  NEW YORK
  OLYMPIA
  RALEIGH
  SAN FRANCISCO

U.S. DYNAMITE CRUISER (1)
  VESUVIUS

U.S. GUNBOAT (2)
  CONCORD
  PETREL

U.S. MONITOR (3)
  MIANTONOMAH
  PURITAN
  TERROR

U.S. RAM (1)
  KATAHDIN

U.S. TORPEDO BOAT (3)
  CUSHING
  ERICSON
  STILETTO

OCEAN LINERS & FERRIES

Issuer Unknown. 1930's. 1¼" cell. BW. No mfr. 17 seen.

CHAUNCEY M. DEPEW
CONTE DI SAVOIA
DE WITT CLINTON
HENDRICK HUDSON
PETER STUYVESANT
QUEEN MARY

ROBERT FULTON
S.S. AMERICANA
S.S. BELLE ISLAND
S.S. MAURETANIA
S.S. MAYFLOWER
S.S. NORMANDIE

S.S. RICHARD PECK
S.S. STATE OF DELAWARE
S.S. WAUKETA
S.S. WESTCHESTER
THE REX

SPACE

Issuer Unknown. Circa 1957. 7/8'' (except as noted) litho. Blue, orange & white; also green, yellow, red & black. Green Duck. 13 seen.

FLYING SAUCERS
MARTIAN
MOON MAN
MUTNIK WOOF WOOF
SATELLITE SPACE SHIP (blue & white) and
   (green & yellow)
SKY OBSERVER SPACE SATELLITE
   OFFICIAL (1⅜'')

SPACE CADET
SPACE RANGER
SPACE RANGERS
SPUTNIK
SPUTNIK SPACE DOG
SPUTNIK SPACE ROCKET
SPUTNIK SPACE WATCHER

SPORTS/GAMES

BASEBALL LEADERS

Issuer Unknown. 1930's. 13/16'' litho. RWB, black & yellow. No mfr. 13 seen.

BIG LEAGUE LEADER
  LONGEST GAME PLAYED   BOSTON VS. BROOKLYN 26 Innings May 11, 1920
  MOST GAMES WON IN A SEASON   CHICAGO N.L.   116 GAMES 1906
  MOST HOME RUNS PER SEASON   BABE RUTH N.Y. AL.   60 IN 1927
  MOST SHUT-OUT GAMES PER SEASON   GROVER ALEXANDER Phila. N.L.
    16 GAMES 1916

AMERICAN LEAGUE LEADER
  BATTING D. ALEXANDER DET. BOS. .367 1932
  BATTING L.A. Fonseca Cleve. .369 1931
  BATTING A.H. Simmons Phila. .390 1931
  PITCHING BOB GROVE PHILA. EARNED RUN AV. 2.84 1932

NATL. LEAGUE LEADER
  BATTING C.J. Hafey St. L. .349 1931
  BATTING Frank J. O'Doul Phila. .398 1929
  HIGHEST PERCENTAGE BATTER SINCE 1900 Rogers Hornsby St. L. N.L. .424
  PITCHING Lon Warneke Chicago Earned Run Av. 2.37 1932
  STOLEN BASES Max Carey Pitts. N.L. Led League for 10 Years.

BASEBALL PLAYERS

Kolb's Mothers' Bread. 1922-1923. 7/8'' cell. BW & red. Bastian. Reading Baseball Club, International League. 32 seen.

SPENCER ABBOTT - MGR.
BABINGTON - F.
BARRETT - INF.
R. BATES - 1B.
CHIEF BENDER - MGR.
M. BROWN - P.
CARTS - P.
CLARKE - C.
T. CONNELLY - F.
GETZ - 2B.
GILHOOLEY - F.
GORDONIER - P.
HAINES - F.
KARPP - P.
J. KELLEY - F
KOTCH - F.

LIGHTNER - R F
LYNN - C.
A. MAMAUX - P.
MARTIN - P.
R. MILLER - 3B.
PAHLMAN - 1B.
SAM POST - 1st B.
AL SCHACHT - P.
SCOTT - INF.
SMALLWOOD - P.
SWARTZ - P.
F. THOMAS - 3B.
M. THOMAS - P.
TRAGESSER - C.
WASHBURN - 2 B.
WOLFE - S.S.

BASEBALL PLAYERS

MLBPA MFG: R-R. 1969. 7/8" litho. BW with blue rims (for National league teams) or red rims (for American League teams). No mfr. **Set of 60,** 30 in each league.

NATIONAL LEAGUE

ATLANTA BRAVES
  HANK AARON
  FELIPE ALOU
  ORLANDO CEPEDA

CHICAGO CUBS
  ERNIE BANKS
  DON KESSINGER
  RON SANTO
  BILLY WILLIAMS

CINCINNATI REDS
  JOHNNY BENCH
  TOMMY HELMS
  JIM MALONEY
  PETE ROSE

HOUSTON ASTROS
  JIM WYNN

LOS ANGELES DODGERS
  WILLY DAVIS
  DON DRYSDALE
  RON FAIRLY

NEW YORK METS
  BUD HARRELSON
  JERRY KOOSMAN
  RON SWOBODA

PHILADELPHIA PHILLIES
  RICHIE ALLEN
  JOHNNY CALLISON

PITTSBURGH PIRATES
  ROBERTO CLEMENTE

ST. LOUIS CARDINALS
  LOU BROCK
  CURT FLOOD
  BOB GIBSON
  TIM McCARVER
  JOE TORRE

SAN FRANCISCO GIANTS
  JIM HART
  JUAN MARICHAL
  WILLIE MAYS
  WILLIE McCOVEY

AMERICAN LEAGUE

BALTIMORE ORIOLES
  BOOG POWELL
  BROOKS ROBINSON
  FRANK ROBINSON

BOSTON RED SOX
  KEN HARRELSON
  JIM LONBORG
  CARL YASTRZEMSKI

CALIFORNIA ANGELS
  GEORGE BRUNET
  JIM FREGOSI
  RICK REICHARDT

CHICAGO WHITE SOX
  LUIS APARICIO
  JOEL HORLEN
  PETE WARD

CLEVELAND INDIANS
MAX ALVIS
TONY HORTON
SAM McDOWELL
LUIS TIANT

DETROIT TIGERS
BILL FREEHAN
WILLIE HORTON
AL KALINE
MICKEY LOLICH
DENNY McLAIN

MINNESOTA TWINS
ROD CAREW
DEAN CHANCE
HARMON KILLEBREW
TONY OLIVA

NEW YORK YANKEES
JOE PEPITONE
MEL STOTTLEMYRE

OAKLAND ATHLETICS
RICK MONDAY

WASHINGTON SENATORS
FRANK HOWARD
PETE RICHERT

BASEBALL PLAYERS

Mrs. Sherlock's Home Made Bread. 1920. 7/8" cell. BW. Bastian. Toledo baseball team. 19 seen.

BRADY - P.
BRESNAHAN - MGR.
DUBUC - P.
DYER - 2B.
FOX - UTILITY
HYATT - 1ST. B.
JONES - S.S.

J. KELLY - C.F.
M. KELLY - C.
KORES - 3B.
McCOLL - P.
McNEILL - C.
MIDDLETON - P.

MURPHY - C.
NELSON - P.
STRYKER - P.
THOMPSON - UTILITY
WICKLAND - R.F.
WILHOIT - L.F.

BASEBALL PLAYERS

Orbit Gum. 1935. 13/16" litho. Green background, names in blue or black on yellow strip. No mfr. Apparently a skip-numbered set. Also issued without numbers. 58 numbered, 58 unnumbered: 116 seen.

1 ANDREWS Boston "Red Sox"
2 REYNOLDS St. Louis "Browns"
3 RIGGS STEPHENSON Chicago "Cubs"
4 WARNEKE Chicago "Cubs"
5 GRUBE Chicago "White Sox"
6 "KIKI" CUYLER Chicago "Cubs"
7 McMANUS Boston "Red Sox"
8 "LEFTY" CLARK Brooklyn "Dodgers"
8 "LEFTY" CLARK New York "Giants"

9 BLAEHOLDER St. Louis "Browns"
10 KAMM Cleveland "Indians"
11 "DYKES" Chicago "White Sox"
12 AVERILL Cleveland "Indians"
13 PAT MALONE Chicago "Cubs"
14 "DIZZY" DEAN St. Louis "Cardinals"
15 BARTELL Phila. "Phillies"
16 GUY BUSH Chicago "Cubs"
17 TINNING Chicago "Cubs"
18 JIMMY FOXX Phila. "Athletics"
19 "MULE" HASS Chicago "White Sox"
20 FONSECA Chicago "White Sox"
21 "PEPPER" MARTIN St. Louis
     "Cardinals"
22 PHIL COLLINS Phila. "Phillies"
23 CISSELL Cleveland "Indians"
24 HADLEY St. Louis "Browns"
25 SMEAD JOLLY Boston "Red Sox"
26 GRIMES Chicago "Cubs"
27 ALEXANDER Boston "Red Sox"
28 COCHRANE Phila. "Athletics"
29 HARDER Cleveland "Indians"
30 MARK KOENIG Chicago "Cubs"
31 "LEFTY" O'DOUL Brooklyn "Dodgers"
31 "LEFTY" O'DOUL New York "Giants"
32 ENGLISH Chicago "Cubs"
32 ENGLISH Chicago "Cubs" (with bat)

33 JURGES Chicago "Cubs"
33 JURGES Chicago "Cubs (with bat)
34 CAMPBELL St. Louis "Browns"
35 VOSMIK Cleveland "Indians"
36 PORTER Cleveland "Indians"
37 CHARLIE GRIMM Chicago "Cubs"
38 GEO. EARNSHAW Phila. "Athletics"
39 AL SIMMONS Chicago "White Sox"
40 "RED" LUCAS Cincinnati "Reds"
51 BERGER Boston "Braves"
55 LEVEY St. Louis "Browns"
58 LOMBARDI Cincinnati "Reds"
64 BURNS St. Louis "Browns"
67 BILLY HERMAN Chicago "Cubs"
72 BILL HALLAHAN St. Louis
     "Cardinals"
92 BRENNAN New York "Yankees"
96 SAM BYRD New York "Yankees"
99 BEN CHAPMAN New York
     "Yankees"
103 JOHN ALLEN New York "Yankees"
107 TONY LAZZERI New York "Yankees"
111 EARL COMBS New York "Yankees"
116 JOE SEWELL New York "Yankees"
120 VERNON GOMEZ New York
     "Yankees"

NOTE: Nos. 26 and 38 have been seen with both blue and black lettering.

The following numbered buttons have been seen unnumbered:

1 ANDREWS	16 BUSH	31 O'DOUL "Dodgers"
2 REYNOLDS	17 TINNING	32 ENGLISH
3 STEPHENSON	18 FOXX	33 JURGES
4 WARNEKE	19 HASS	35 VOSMIK
5 GRUBE	20 FONSECA	36 PORTER
6 CUYLER	21 MARTIN	37 GRIMM
7 McMANUS	22 COLLINS	38 EARNSHAW
8 CLARK "Dodgers"	23 CISSELL	39 SIMMONS
9 BLAEHOLDER	24 HADLEY	40 LUCAS
10 KAMM	25 JOLLY	51 BERGER
11 "DYKES"	26 GRIMES	58 LOMBARDI
12 AVERILL	27 ALEXANDER	64 BURNS
13 MALONE	28 COCHRANE	67 HERMAN
14 DEAN	29 HARDER	72 HALLAHAN
15 BARTELL	30 KOENIG	

Following are unnumbered buttons that have not been seen with numbers:

"LEFTY" GROVE Phila. "Athletics"
"CHICK" HAFEY Cincinnati "Reds"
HAINES St. Louis "Cardinals"
"GABBY" HARTNETT Chicago "Cubs"
"BABE" HERMAN Chicago "Cubs"
HORNSBY St. Louis "Cardinals"
JOHNSON Boston "Red Sox"

TED LYONS Chicago "White Sox"
CONNIE MACK Mgr. of Phila. "A's"
ROOT Chicago "Cubs"
SEEDS Boston "Red Sox"
WALBERG Phila. "Athletics"
PAUL WANER Pittsburgh "Pirates"
WHITNEY Phila. "Phillies"

BASEBALL PLAYERS

  **Sweet Caporal Cigarettes.** 1910-1911. 7/8" cell. BW or brown & white. W&H. Two different series, one with larger letters and sometimes with a different picture. *After name means that the button appeared in both series. **Set of 204.**

BOSTON RED SOX (10)
Carrigan*
Cicotte
Engle*
Hooper
Karger
Speaker*
Wagner

BOSTON RUSTLERS (5)
Abbaticchio
Ferguson
Herzog
Mattern*

BROOKLYN SUPERBAS (13)
Barger
Bell*
Bergen
Dahlen
Erwin
Hummel
Rucker*
Scanlon
Smith
Wheat*

CHICAGO CUBS (19)
Archer*
Brown*
Chance*
Evers
Kroh
McIntire
Needham
Overall
Pfiester
Reulbach
Richie
Schulte
Sheckard
Steinfeldt
Tinker*

CHICAGO WHITE SOX (11)
Callahan
Dougherty
Duffy*
Lord*
McIntyre*
Parent
Walsh
White

CINCINNATI REDS (15)
Bates
Beebe
Bescher
Downey*
Fromme
Gaspar
Grant
Griffith
Clark Griffith
Hoblitzell
McLean*
Mitchell
Suggs

CLEVELAND NAPS (8)
Ball
Birmingham
Lajoie
Stovall*
Turner
"Cy" Young
Old Cy Young

DETROIT TIGERS (14)
  Cobb
  "Ty" Cobb
  Delahanty
  Donovan
  Jennings*
  Tom Jones
  Killian
  Mullen
  Mullin
  O'Leary
  Schmidt*
  Stanage

NEW YORK GIANTS (22)
  Ames
  Becker
  Bridwell
  Crandall
  Devlin
  Devore
  Doyle*
  Drucke
  Herzog
  Latham
  Marquard
  Mathewson*
  McGraw*
  Merkle
  "Chief" Meyers
  Murray*
  Wilson
  Wiltse

NEW YORK YANKEES (11)
  Chase*
  Cree
  Ford*
  Hemphill
  Knight*
  Quinn
  Warhop
  Wolter

PHILA. ATHLETICS (14)
  Baker
  Barry
  Bender
  "Chief" Bender
  Collins
  Eddie Collins
  Dygert
  Hartsel
  Krause
  Livingston
  Murphy
  Oldring
  Thomas
  Ira Thomas

PHILA. PHILLIES (13)
  Bransfield
  Dooin*
  Doolan*
  Lobert
  Magee
  Moran
  Paskert*
  Rowan
  Titus*

PITTSBURG(H) PIRATES (16)
  Byrne
  Camnitz*
  Clarke
  Fred Clarke
  Flynn
  Gibson*
  Leach
  Tommy Leach
  Leever
  Leifield
  Maddox
  Miller
  Phillippe
  Wilson

ST. LOUIS BROWNS (10)
  Austin*
  Hoffman
  La Porte*
  Pelty
  Stone
  Wallace*
  Wallace (no cap)

ST. LOUIS CARDINALS (12)
  Bresnahan*
  Bresnahan (diff. pic.)
  Evans
  Harmon
  Hauser
  Huggins*
  Konetchy
  Oakes*
  Phelps

WASHINGTON SENATORS (11)
  Elberfeld*
  Gray
  Groom
  Johnson*
  McBride
  Milan
  Schaefer
  Street*

51

BASEBALL PLAYERS

Topps Chewing Gum. 1956. 1⅜₁₆″ litho. MC. No mfr. Offered as a set of 90, but only 60 were issued. **Set of 60.**

BALTIMORE ORIOLES
 CHUCK DIERING of
 WILLIE MIRANDA ss
 HAL SMITH c
 GUS TRIANDOS 1b

BOSTON RED SOX
 GRADY HATTON 3b
 JACKIE JENSEN of
 FRANK SULLIVAN p
 TED WILLIAMS of

BROOKLYN DODGERS
 SANDY AMOROS of
 GIL HODGES 1b
 JACKIE ROBINSON 3b
 DUKE SNIDER of
 KARL SPOONER p

CHICAGO CUBS
 ERNIE BANKS ss
 HANK SAUER of
 BILL TREMEL p

CHICAGO WHITE SOX
 DICK DONOVAN p
 JACK HARSHMAN p
 BOB KENNEDY 3b
 JIM RIVERA of

CINCINNATI REDLEGS
 JOE BLACK p
 ART FOWLER p
 TED KLUSZEWSKI 1b
 ROY McMILLAN ss

CLEVELAND INDIANS
 JIM HEGAN c
 DON MOSSI p
 AL ROSEN 3b
 AL SMITH of

DETROIT TIGERS
 RAY BOONE 3b
 FRANK HOUSE c
 AL KALINE of

KANSAS CITY ATHLETICS
 JIM FINIGAN 2b
 HECTOR LOPEZ 3b
 VIC POWER 1b
 GUS ZERNIAL of

MILWAUKEE BRAVES
 HANK AARON of
 GENE CONLEY p
 ED MATHEWS 3b
 WARREN SPAHN p

NEW YORK GIANTS
 RUBEN GOMEZ p
 BOBBY HOFMAN if
 WILLIE MAYS of

NEW YORK YANKEES
 YOGI BERRA c
 JOE COLLINS 1b
 PHIL RIZZUTO ss
 BILL SKOWRON 1b
 BOB TURLEY p

PHILADELPHIA PHILLIES
 RON NEGRAY p
 MAYO SMITH m
 HERMAN WEHMEIER p

PITTSBURGH PIRATES
 DICK GROAT ss
 DALE LONG 1b
 JOHNNY O'BRIEN 2b

ST. LOUIS CARDINALS
 LUIS ARROYO p
 KEN BOYER 3b
 HARVEY HADDIX p
 WALLY MOON of

WASHINGTON NATIONALS
 CARLOS PAULA of
 ROY SIEVERS of
 CHUCK STOBBS p

BASEBALL PLAYERS

Ward's Sporties. 1930's. 1¼'' cell. BW & red or blue, white & red. No mfr. 8 seen.

DIZZY DEAN	CHARLIE GEHRINGER
JIMMIE DYKES	CHARLIE GRIMM
JIMMIE FOXX	SCHOOLBOY ROWE
FRANK FRISCH	JIMMIE WILSON

BASEBALL PLAYERS

Issuer Unknown. 1930's. 13/16'' litho. Blue, white, yellow & flesh. No mfr. **Set of 25.**

CHARLES BERRY	GEORGE GRANTHAM	CARL RAYNOLDS
"BILL" CISSELL	"CHARLEY" GRIMM	CHARLES RUFFING
"KIKI" CUYLER	"LEFTY" GROVE	"AL" SIMMONS
"DIZZY" DEAN	"GABBY" HARTNETT	GUS SUHR
WESLEY FERRELL	TRAVIS JACKSON	"BILL" TERRY
FRANK FRISCH	TONY LAZZERI	"DAZZY" VANCE
LOU GEHRIG	"TED" LYONS	PAUL WANER
VERNON GOMEZ	"RABBIT" MARANVILLE	LON WARNEKE
"GOOSE" GOSLIN		

CAUTION: Inks used to print this series are water soluble—buttons cannot be cleaned without risk of losing picture.

BASEBALL PLAYERS

Issuer Unknown. 1910's. 1¹/₁₆'' high oval cell. in ornate brass frame. Sepia. No mfr. 9 seen.

ARCHER	EVERS	MATHEWSON
TY COBB	HOBLITZEL	SPEAKER
AL DEMAREE	LAJOIE	JOE TINKER

BASEBALL POSITIONS

Issued early in the history of pinbacks by various companies, including The Pittsburgh Times, Mancels & Schmidt's Bread, H.B. Windrath of Buffalo, N.Y., Dispatch & Pioneer Press, Harrisburg Athletic Club, Reis' Drugs, Spartana drink and Culvert Bros. Sporting Goods. 7/8″ and 1¼″ cell. BW and MC, many on gold backgrounds. Mfrs. include Baltimore Badge, Bastian, Ehrman, Miller, Pulver and W&H.

BASEBALL POSITIONS

Issuer Unknown. 1930's. 13/16″ litho. MC. No mfr. Seen with lettering in red, black, blue or green. While it is to be expected that buttons enough to comprise two full teams were issued, we list only those we have verified. 19 seen.

GREEN SOX	BLUE SOX
CAPTAIN	CAPTAIN
CATCHER	CATCHER
CENTER FIELD	CENTER FIELD
FIRST BASE	FIRST BASE
LEFT FIELD	LEFT FIELD
PITCHER	PITCHER
RIGHT FIELD	RIGHT FIELD
SECOND BASE	SECOND BASE
SHORT STOP	SHORT STOP
THIRD BASE	

BASEBALL TEAMS

Unless someone somewhere has been collecting and annotating Baseball Team buttons for the past 60 years or so, a sensible listing can probably never be done. There have been lithos, celluloids, and tabs—ranging from 3/4″ to 3½″ and probably larger. They're still being made and sold at the Major League ballparks to this day. **American Nut & Chocolate Co.** issued an early set, as did **"Double Play" Candy, Crane Potato Chips,** and **Guy's Potato Chips,** as well as any number of other advertisers. More recently, and not in such great profusion, Football, Hockey and Basketball Team buttons have appeared. We would welcome help from anyone who has complete sets of Team buttons and who can identify the companies that issued them. In the meantime, happy collecting!

BOXING

Issuer Unknown. 1940's-1960's. 1¾'' cell. BW. No mfr. These were probably made for sale outside arenas at fight time, thus they may not be a set in the true sense. But they have the appearance of a series, and they are interesting in themselves, so we include them. 22 seen.

HENRY ARMSTRONG (2 diff.)
EZZARD CHARLES
CASSIUS CLAY
BILLY CONN
INGEMAR JOHANSSON
SONNY LISTON
JOE LOUIS
JOE LOUIS WORLD'S CHAMPION (2 diff.)

ROCKY MARCIANO
TAMI MAURIELLO
WORLD CHAMPION BOB
  MONTGOMERY
ARCHIE MOORE
PUGILIST LOU NOVA
WILLIE PEP
SUGAR RAY ROBINSON (2 diff.)
MAX SCHMELING
RANDY TURPIN
JERSEY JOE WALCOTT
JERSEY (JOE) WALCOTT

HORSE RACING

High Admiral Cigarette. Circa 1900. 7/8'' cell. MC. Riley-Klotz. 20 seen.

A. HAMILTON JOCKEY EASTONS
  COLORS.
AUG. BELMONT COLORS.
BALLARD, JOCKEY. MADISON STABLES
  COLORS.
BLAKE, JOCKEY. W. JENNINGS COLORS.
C. SLOAN, JOCKEY WALCOT COLORS.
DUKE OF PORTLAND. COLORS.
DWYER COLORS.
ED CORRIGAN COLORS.
E.H. CARRISON, JOCKEY. J. RUPPERT
  COLORS.
FRED TARAL, JOCKEY. MARCUS DALY
  COLORS

GEO. TAYLOR, JOCKEY. J. McLOUGHLIN
  COLORS
H.R.H. PRINCE OF WALES, COLORS.
HY. GRIFFIN, JOCKEY. GIDION & DALY
  COLORS.
J.B. HAGGIN COLORS
MART. BERGEN, JOCKEY KEENE
  COLORS
PIERRE LORILLARD. COLORS.
P. McDERMOTT JOCKEY FRED LOWE
  COLORS
SAM'L DOGGETT, JOCKEY. ONECK
  STABLES COLORS.
SLOAN, JOCKEY. J. CAMPBELL COLORS.
W. SIMS, JOCKEY. R. CROCKER COLORS.

HORSE RACING

Little Jockey Cigarette. Circa 1900. 7/8" cell. MC. W&H. 9 seen.

BARRETT, CELEBRATED ENGLISH JOCKEY.

BERGEN, CELEBRATED AMERICAN JOCKEY.*

DOGGETT, CELEBRATED AMERICAN JOCKEY.

HAMILTON, CELEBRATED AMERICAN JOCKEY.

*Color variety seen.

LOATES, CELEBRATED ENGLISH JOCKEY.*

OSBORNE CELEBRATED ENGLISH JOCKEY.*

SIMS, CELEBRATED AMERICAN JOCKEY.

TARAL CELEBRATED AMERICAN JOCKEY.

WEBB, CELEBRATED ENGLISH JOCKEY.

NOTE: Also seen with American Pepsin Gum backpaper.

MARBLES

Harrisburg Telegraph. 1920's-1930's. 1½" (except as noted) cell. BW & various colors. W&H. 7 seen.

1927 (picture, no name) I AM IN THE TOURNAMENT
1928 "CHAPPIE" REIDELL 6th ANNUAL TOURNAMENT
1929 GLADYS COLEMAN   Seventh Annual Tournament
1930 CURTIS BANKS   Eighth Annual Tournament
1931 EARL FOLLETT Ninth Annual Tournament
1932 (picture, no name) TENTH MARBLE TOURNAMENT
1933 (picture, no name) 11TH MARBLE TOURNAMENT*

*1⁵/₈" x 1¹/₄" oval.

THEATER

ACTRESSES

High Admiral Cigarette. Circa 1900. 7/8" cell. Brown & white. Riley-Klotz. 5 seen.

HOPE BOOTH	RAVEN DU KLOW
LOTTIE COLLINS	CHRISTIE MACDONALD
CORINNE	

ACTRESSES

High Admiral Cigarette. Circa 1900. 1¼" cell. BW. W&H. Comic sayings with photos of unidentified actresses or boxers. 13 seen.

Ah There	It's Naughty But It's Nice
Am I In It (Bob Fitzsimmons)	Now You Stop
Ask Me And Find Out	Oh Mamma Buy Me That
Don't Bother Me (Jack Johnson)	Sweet 16 Aber Nit
Don't Stare At Me	Why Don't You
Give Me a Carmen Kiss	Why Don't You Smile for a Change
If You Love Me Wink	

ACTRESSES

Sweet Caporal Cigarette. Circa 1900. 7/8" cell. Sepia. W&H. Figures in parentheses indicate the number of different portraits seen of that actress. Some buttons in this series were also issued with filled backs, in 7/8" and 15/16", but these have not been tabulated. 252 seen.

Maude Adams (3)	Clara Bell	Helen T. Boucicault (2)
Clairesse Agnew	Bessie Bellwood	Louise Boucicault
Viola Allen (2)	Olive Berkley	Madeline Bouton (2)
Mary Anderson (2)	Sarah Bernhardt	Anna Boyd
Emily Banker (2)	Helen Bertram	Rose Braham
Fanny Batchelder	Amelia Bingham	Mrs. Brown Potter (2)
Helen Beaumont	Mrs. Ballington Booth	Marie Burroughs (2)
Grace Wallace Belasco	Hope Booth (2)	Laura Burt

Amy Busby (3)
Calve
Beatrice Cameron (3)
Bessie Carl
Jessie Carlisle (2)
Carmencita
Louise Leslie Carter
Georgie Cayvan
Kitty Cheatham (3)
Estelle Clayton (2)
Maggie Cline
Lottie Collins
Nanette Comstock
Miss Consuelo
Corinne (4)
Camille D'Arville (2)
Fanny Davenport (2)
Camille De Arville (2)
Violet Defreis
Zellie De Lussan
Gleo De Merode
Dorothy Dene
Dorothy Denning
Clementine De Vere (2)
De Vries
Deyo (4)
Viola Doll
Teddie Du Coe
Alice Dufresne
Virginia Earle (2)
Mabel Eaton
Paula Edwardes (3)
Sophie Elliot
Maxine Elliott
Agnes Evans
Alice Evans
Isabel Eversson (2)
Nina Farrington
Cissy Fitzgerald (4)
Katherine Florence (2)
Mlle. Fougere
Della Fox (4)
Pauline French
Trixie Friganza
Loie Fuller
Johanna Gadski
Minna Gale
Sylvia Gerrish
Bettina Girard

Lulu Glazer (4)
Amelia Glover (2)
Jennie Goldthwaite
Louise Grans
Catherine Grey
Yvette Guilbert
Pauline Hall (2)
Caroline Hamilton
Mary Hampton
Percy Haswell
Anna Held
Flo Henderson
Edna W. Hopper (4)
Birdie Irving
Isabel Irving (3)
Marie Jansen
Maud Jeffries
Fanny Johnson
Jennie Joyce
Emma Juch
Frankie Kemble
Mrs. Kendal
Kathryn Kidder
Grace Kimball (2)
Sadie Kirby
Villa Knox
Lily Landon (2)
Eleanor Lane-Bell
Lily Langtry (2)
Larive
Madge Lessing
Clara Lipman
Mabel Love (2)
Jennette Lowrie
Laura S. Mapleson
Julia Marlow (5)
Sadie Martinot (5)
Blanch Massey
Eleanor Mayo (2)
Agnes Miller
Caroline Miskel (3)
Louise Montague
Helen Nadine
Olga Nethersole
Annie O'Keep
Omene
Elita Proctor Otis
Ffolliet Paget
Edith Palliser

Esther Palliser
Mannine Palmer (2)
Minnie Palmer
Patti
Annie Pixley
Tennye Poole
Phyllis Rankin
Zelma Rawlston
Ada Reeve (2)
Ada Rehan
Margaret Reid (2)
Lillian Relma (2)
Pearl Revare (2)
Rhea
Fanny Rice
Adele Ritchie
Lillian Russell (5)
Josie Sadler
Jeanette St. Henry
Maud St. John
Annie St. Tel
Minnie Seligman (2)
Effie Shannon
Lizzie Sherwood
Marie D. Shotwell (2)
Kate Stokes
Kate Stuart
Marie Studholme (3)
Anna Suits
Annie Sutherland
Marie Tempest (2)
Fay Templeton
Ellaline Terriss (2)
Ellen Terry
Charlotte Tittel
Carrie Turner
Odette Tyler
Bessie Tyree
Qeenie Vassar
Theresa Vaughan (4)
Irene Vera
The Misses Volk
Marie Wainwright
Gladys Wallis
Blanch Walsh
Fanny Ward (2)
Clara Weiland
Sybil Wyndham

TV/RADIO

AMOS 'N' ANDY

Amos 'n' Andy Fresh Air Candy. 1930's. 13/16" litho.
Black & yellow. Greenduck or no mfr. 18 seen.

Amos 'n' Andy Fresh Air Candy (taxi)
BE MY RUBY TAYLOR
DON'T GET SARCASTIC
FREE RIDE IN FRESH AIR TAXI
  WAIT ON ANY CORNER
HELLO BIG BOY
HOWDY BOYS
HOW IS YOU KINGFISH
I AIN'T GOIN DO IT
I LOVES YOU HONEY
IMA GOLD-FISH WHAT R.U.
  MYSTIC KNIGHTS OF THE SEA

IMA KING-FISH WHAT R.U.
  MYSTIC KNIGHTS OF THE SEA
IMA SARDINE WHAT R.U.
  MYSTIC KNIGHTS OF THE SEA
IMA SHARK WHAT R.U.
  MYSTIC KNIGHTS OF THE SEA
IMA SUCKER WHAT R.U.
  MYSTIC KNIGHTS OF THE SEA
I 2NDS DE MOTION
I'SE DE PRESIDENT
I'SE REGUSTED
OH! OH! AIN'T THAT SUMPIN

BATMAN

N.P.P. Inc. (National Periodical Publications) 1966.
15/16" litho. MC. Creative House. **Set of 14,** plus color
varieties.

BATMAN
CALLING BATMAN!
DICK GRAYSON ROBIN
HOLY RAVIOLI ZOK!
I AM A BATMAN FAN
I'M A BATMAN CRIMEFIGHTER
ROBIN
STOP THEM ROBIN! WHA-RAMM!

THE BATMAN BRUCE WAYNE
THE BATMAN BRUCE WAYNE
  (small type)
THE BATMOBILE
THE JOKER
THE RIDDLER
YOU'VE DONE IT AGAIN
  BOY WONDER POW!

BATMAN

N.P.P. Inc. (National Periodical Publications) 1966. 1″ litho. MC. Creative House. 15 seen, plus color varieties.

BATMAN   BRUCE WAYNE
BATMAN   POW
BATMAN   ZOP
BATMOBILE
BATWOMAN
CALLING BATMAN!
I AM A BATMAN CRIMEFIGHTER
I AM A BATMAN FAN

MEMBER BATMAN BUTTON CLUB
OFFICIAL BATMAN MEMBER*
PENGUIN
ROBIN
ROBIN   DICK GRAYSON
THE JOKER
THE RIDDLER

*Issued with LP record package but appears to belong to this set.

GREEN HORNET

Greenway Prod. Inc., Twentieth Century-Fox Tel. Inc.
1966. 7/8″ litho. BW, green & red. Green Duck. 9 seen.

BLACK BEAUTY
HORNET GAS GUN
HORNET STING
KATO
MISS CASE   THE GREEN HORNET'S
   SECRETARY

THE GREEN HORNET (hornet)
THE GREEN HORNET (man)
THE GREEN HORNET FAN
THE GREEN HORNET'S FLASHLIGHT
   & POCKET WATCH

HUCKLEBERRY HOUND

Hanna-Barbera Prod. 1964. 15/16'' litho. MC. Green Duck. 18 seen, plus color varieties.

BOO-BOO SAYS WHO ELSE YOGI AND HUCK
DROOPY FOR VICE-PRES.
FOR HUCK HOUND PRESIDENT
FOR PRESIDENT AND VICE PRES. (Magilla - Droopy Jugate)
FOR PRESIDENT MAGILLA DROOPY FOR VICE PRESIDENT
GIRLS VOTE FOR MAGILLA & DROOPY
HUCK HOUND FOR PRESIDENT
HUCK HOUND FOR VICE PRESIDENT
HUCKLEBERRY HOUND FOR VICE PRESIDENT
I'M FOR MAGILLA for PRESIDENT
I'M FOR YOGI AND HUCK HOUND
MAGILLA GORILLA for PRESIDENT
MR. JINKS THINKS IN '64 IT'S YOGI & HUCK ALL THE WAY
YOGI BEAR for PRESIDENT (2 diff.)
YOGI BEAR FOR PRESIDENT AND HUCK VICE PRES.
YOGI BEAR FOR PRESIDENT WAKE UP AMERICA
YOGI for President HUCK FOR VICE PRESIDENT

JACKIE GLEASON

VIP Corp. 1955. 1¼'' and 1¾'' cell. BW photos and one color. No mfr. Each button appears in the two sizes. **Set of 14.**

AND "AW-A-A-Y WE GO"
JOE THE BARTENDER
MMMM! BOY
REGGIE VAN GLEASON THE III

THE BUS DRIVER
THE LOUD-MOUTH
THE POOR SOUL

RED BUTTONS

Issuer Unknown. 1950's. 1½" cell. BW & red. Emress. Each button has a BW portrait in center (described below), RED BUTTONS around bottom, and HEE-HEE HO-HO HOO-HOO around top. 11 seen.

Boxer
Cowboy hat
Derby hat
Smiling
  (same picture, larger)

Smiling with finger raised
  (same picture, larger)
Wool-knit cap
  (same picture in grey circle)
Wrinkling nose
  (same picture, larger)

ROOTIE KAZOOTIE CLUB

R.K. Inc. 1950's. 1⅛" litho. MC. No mfr. 6 seen.

EL SQUEAKO MOUSE
GALA-POOCHIE PUP
MR. DEETLE DOOTLE

POISON ZOOMACK
POLKA DOTTIE
ROOTIE KAZOOTIE

ROOTIE KAZOOTIE CLUB

TELU. 1950's. 1⅛" litho. BW. Olympic Button & Emblem. 6 seen.

"BIG TODD" RUSSELL
EL SQUEAKO
LITTLE NIPPER*

POISON ZOOMACK
ROOTIE KAZOOTIE

Two varieties: one with RCA on curl, one with RCA on face.

ROWAN & MARTIN'S LAUGH-IN

George Schlatter - Ed Friendly Productions & Romart Inc. 1969. 7/8'' litho. 3 colors. CHP Chicago. 22 seen, plus color varieties.

PORTRAITS (BW on one color)

RUTH BUZZI
JUDY CARNE
HENRY GIBSON
ARTE JOHNSON

DICK MARTIN
DAN ROWAN
JOANNE WORLEY

SAYINGS (MC)

DUMB DUMB DUMB
FLYING FICKLE FINGER OF FATE
GO TO YOUR ROOM
HERE COMES THE JUDGE
HEY SMARTY — LET'S PARTY
HOW DOES THAT GRAB YOU
I'M MOD ABOUT U
RING MY CHIMES

SOCK IT TO ME
THAT'S A NO-NO
VERRY INNTERESTING
YOU BET YOUR SWEET BIPPY
YOU'RE MY DING A LING
YOU'RE MY THING!
YOU ZING ME

VICTORIANA

ART SCENES

Cameo Pepsin Gum and **El Capitan Chewing Gum.** Circa 1898. 1¼" cell. MC, except as noted. W&H. Apparently adaptations of paintings popular at the end of the 19th century. No titles or identification. (Also seen with W&H backpaper and with backpaper of Norristown Fire Dept., Nov. 24, 1898, parade). 18 seen.

Cherub kissing woman
Cherub & woman warming their hands
Couple running with raised cape
Deer
Dog at rest
Farm couple praying in field
Five young winged heads
Girl, cat & dog watching frog
Heads of three white stallions

Kitten in a boot
Muzzled puppy*
Naked child & dog on pier
Nymph kneeling on rock
Pensive cherub
Retriever with bird in mouth
Woman prostrate on cross
Young girl praying

Also seen in sepia with title: FOR THE SAFETY OF THE PUBLIC.

CAMEOS

Cameo Pepsin Gum. Circa 1900. 1¼" cell. Ivory & black or ivory & pink. W&H. No text, no identification. 3 seen.

WOMEN'S PORTRAITS

Issuers include **Athletic All Tobacco, Chesterfield Cigarettes, Cracker Jack, The Favorite Cigarettes, International Tailoring Co., Napoleon All Tobacco, Paw-Paw Girl, Perfection Cigarettes, Pick Plug Cut Tobacco,** and **Woodward Co.** (Wines & Whiskies). Circa 1905-1909. 7/8" and 1¼" cell. MC. W&H. Idealized female beauties in porcelain-like colors. No names. 27 of the 7/8" and 25 of the 1¼" have been seen, as well as various size oval stickpins.

WESTERN

DAVY CROCKETT

Issuer unknown. 1950's. 13/16" litho. Various 2-color combinations. No mfr. (MADE IN U.S.A. on curl.) 8 seen.

DAVY CROCKETT		DAVY CROCKETT	INDIAN FIGHTER
DAVY CROCKETT	BEAR KILLER	DAVY CROCKETT	INDIAN SCOUT
DAVY CROCKETT	CONGRESSMAN	DAVY CROCKETT	JUNIOR SCOUT
DAVY CROCKETT	FRONTIER SCOUT	DAVY CROCKETT	STATESMAN

THE LONE RANGER

Buchan's Bread. 1940's. 7/8" or 1¼" cell. Various colors. No mfr. 8 seen.

"HI-YO SILVER"	LONE RANGER LOAF (only one with
"LONE RANGER"	picture—shows bread loaf)
Lone Ranger Community Safety Club	"MASKED RIDER"
DEPUTY (1¼")	"SCOUT"
Lone Ranger Community Safety Club	"SILVER BULLET"
MEMBER (1¼")	

ROY ROGERS

Post's Grape-Nuts Flakes. 1953. 7/8" litho (plus one 1¼"). MC. No mfr. Set also exists without Grape-Nuts or other identification on back, possibly distributed in gumball machines. Also seen: a 1⅝" ROY ROGERS with Post's copyright on back. **Set of 16.**

BULLET	ROY ROGERS	ROY'S BOOTS
BUTTERMILK	ROY ROGERS (1¼")	ROY'S BRAND RR
DALE EVANS	ROY ROGERS JUNIOR	ROY'S GUNS
DALE'S BRAND DE	DEPUTY	ROY—TRIGGER
NELLYBELLE	ROY ROGERS' SADDLE	TRIGGER
PAT BRADY	ROY ROGERS SHERIFF	

TOM MIX RALSTON STRAIGHT SHOOTERS

Ralston Cereal. 1946. 1″ litho. BW & red. No mfr. Code words on reverse, in parentheses below. **Set of 5.**

RALSTON STRAIGHT SHOOTERS

    JANE (TOMORROW)
    MIKE SHAW (NO)
    TONY (GUILTY)
    WASH (DANGER AHEAD)

TOM MIX OF RADIO

    CURLEY BRADLEY (YES)

COWBOYS

Issuer Unknown. Circa 1955. 7/8″ litho. BW or brown picture on single-color background. Green Duck. Some have name of star on reverse (given in parentheses below). Others have Green Duck identification on reverse. 14 seen, plus color varieties.

GENE AUTRY
JIM BOWIE
BUFFALO BILL, JR.
CHAMPION
CHEYENNE (Clint Walker)
COLT-45 (Wayde Preston)
BRAVE EAGLE*

WILD BILL HICKOK
JINGLES
ANNIE OAKLEY
THE LONE RANGER
THE RANGE RIDER
SUGARFOOT (Will Hutchins)
RIN TIN TIN

* © 1955 *ROY ROGERS ENTERPRISES INC. on curl.*

COWBOYS

Issuer Unknown. 1940's - 1950's. 1¼" cell. BW or MC. No mfr. These buttons comprise a set only in their theme and in the similarity of design over the years. Among the cowboys are:

GENE AUTRY (8 diff.)	DALE EVANS (3 diff.)	ALLAN "ROCKY" LANE
ROD CAMERON (2 diff.)	MONTE HALE (2 diff.)	(2 diff.)
HOPALONG CASSIDY	GEORGE "GABBY" HAYES	JOHNNY MACK BROWN
(3 diff.)	(3 diff.)	ROY ROGERS (5 diff.)
NANCY CHAMBERS	WILD BILL HICKOK	CHARLES STARRETT (2 diff.)
ANDY CLYDE	TIM HOLT	JOHN WAYNE
BUSTER CRABBE	JINGLES	WHIP WILSON (2 diff.)

INDIANS

American Pepsin Gum. Circa 1900. 7/8" cell. MC. W&H. Each issued in two varieties: one with red lettering, the other with blue lettering. 12 seen.

BLACK EYE. BLACKFEET SIOUX.	RUSHING BEAR. PAWNEE.
LEAN WOLF. GROS VENTRES.	SITTING BULL DAKOTA SIOUX.
RED CLOUD, DAKOTA SIOUX.	SPOTTED TAIL BLACKFEET SIOUX.

INDIANS

Issuer Unknown. 1930's. 13/16" litho. Blue, white, yellow & flesh. No mfr. 11 seen.

JOSEPH BRANT	OSCEOLA	TECUMSEH
KING PHILIP	RED CLOUD	WEASEL CALF
KING PHILIPP	RED JACKET	WHITE CAP
MASSASOIT	SOUNDING SKY	

CAUTION: Inks used to print this series are water-soluble—buttons cannot be cleaned without risk of losing picture.

INDIANS & WESTERN

Van Brode. 1950's. 1³/₈'' litho. MC but mainly brown & red. No mfr. Short biographies on reverse. **Numbered set of 10.**

1. BUFFALO BILL CODY
2. CHIEF PONTIAC
3. DAVEY CROCKETT
4. BLACK HAWK SAUK INDIAN CHIEF
5. KING PHILIP

6. CHRISTOPHER KIT CARSON
7. GERONIMO
8. SITTING BULL
9. DANIEL BOONE
10. TECUMSEH SHAWNEE

WESTERN & MILITARY HEROES

Issuer Unknown. 1930's. 13/16'' litho. Blue, white, yellow & flesh. No mfr. 11 seen.

CAPT. D. L. PAYNE
CAPT. MERIWETHER LEWIS
CAPT. WILLIAM CLARK
DANIEL BOONE
DAVID CROCKET
DAVID CROCKETT

GEN. ISRAEL PUTNAM
GEN. WM. S. HARNEY
KIT CARSON
WHITE BEAVER
WILD BILL HICKOK

CAUTION: Inks used to print this series are water-soluble—buttons cannot be cleaned without risk of losing picture.

THE BUTTON BOOK
REVISED PRICES

The following list revises the prices for each button illustrated in the 1972 edition of *The Button Book*. The prices are for buttons in extremely fine condition. Additional considerations used to arrive at prices are: 1) amount of collector interest in a particular button category, 2) the scarcity of the button, 3) the design quality, 4) whether the button is pictorial or just a slogan, 5) its age, and 6) its size. Buttons with obvious stains, scratches, cuts or rim splits are worth substantially less than full value.

The prices specified are nationwide average retail prices. This means most of the collectors for a particular button category would be willing to pay the prices indicated. Collectors with specialized interests, those trying to complete a set, and collectors in areas where there is much competition may be willing to pay a bit more. However, there is an equal number of collectors at the opposite end of the price spectrum.

In the case of buttons issued as a set, the price given applies only to the one example button illustrated in *The Button Book*. Usually, other buttons in the same set will have approximately the same value, but this is not always the case. For example, particularly popular comic characters or baseball players will command a higher price than the less popular characters or players in the set.

All values specified are approximations and the publisher shall not be held responsible for losses that may occur in the purchase or sale of items.

SECTION I
CELEBRITIES

I-A Events
1 - 35
2 - 20
3 - 20
4 - 8
5 - 12
6 - 12
7 - 4
8 - 5
9 - 4

I-B Holidays
1 - 8
2 - 12
3 - 10
4 - 8
5 - 8
6 - 5
7 - 5
8 - 10

I-C Santa Claus
1 - 60
2 - 40
3 - 30
4 - 20
5 - 20
6 - 20
7 - 35
8 - 20
9 - 12
10 - 4
11 - 4
12 - 8

SECTION II
ENTERTAINMENT

II-A Amusement Parks
1 - 35
2 - 8
3 - 20
4 - 35

II-B Circus
1 - 10
2 - 5
3 - 8
4 - 5
5 - 5
6 - 3
7 - 15

II-C Comic Characters
1 - 15
2 - 12
3 - 8
4 - 25
5 - 10
6 - 6
7 - 12
8 - 8
9 - 5
10 - 8
11 - 18
12 - 4
13 - 2
14 - 4
15 - 8
16 - 2
17 - 20
18 - 10
19 - 2
20 - 35
21 - 45
22 - 45
23 - 100
24 - 35
25 - 35
26 - 50
27 - 25
28 - 40
29 - 75
30 - 40
31 - 20
32 - 20
33 - 20
34 - 20
35 - 60
36 - 75
37 - 15
38 - 100
39 - 75
40 - 25
41 - 15
42 - 20
43 - 25
44 - 15
45 - 12
46 - 5
47 - 10
48 - 6
49 - 3
50 - 20
51 - 20
52 - 100
53 - 8
54 - 12
55 - 12
56 - 12
57 - 12
58 - 18
59 - 5
60 - 15
61 - 3

II-D Cowboys
1 - 30
2 - 20
3 - 10
4 - 35
5 - 8
6 - 75
7 - 10
8 - 5
9 - 10
10 - 15
11 - 12
12 - 5
13 - 15
14 - 20
15 - 6
16 - 5
17 - 10
18 - 20
19 - 6

II-E Movies
1 - 20
2 - 30
3 - 10
4 - 15
5 - 100
6 - 50
7 - 3
8 - 50
9 - 50
10 - 80
11 - 50
12 - 30
13 - 20
14 - 20
15 - 15
16 - 20
17 - 20
18 - 15
19 - 6
20 - 15
21 - 12
22 - 20
23 - 6
24 - 8
25 - 8
26 - 8
27 - 8
28 - 5
29 - 4
30 - 8
31 - 15
32 - 25
33 - 50
34 - 30
35 - 35
36 - 50
37 - 20
38 - 20
39 - 12
40 - 12
41 - 8
42 - 8

II-F Musicians
1 - 10
2 - 8
3 - 5
4 - 15

II-G Radio
1 - 8
2 - 5
3 - 6
4 - 5
5 - 5
6 - 5
7 - 5
8 - 4
9 - 8
10 - 4
11 - 3
12 - 12
13 - 8
14 - 15
15 - 4
16 - 8
17 - 10
18 - 60
19 - 8
20 - 5
21 - 5
22 - 8
23 - 25
24 - 3
25 - 3
26 - 5
27 - 12

II-H Singers
1 - 5
2 - 15
3 - 10
4 - 8
5 - 15
6 - 6
7 - 4

II-I Television
1 - 6
2 - 15
3 - 8
4 - 8
5 - 3
6 - 2
7 - 2
8 - 5
9 - 4
10 - 3
11 - 10

II-J Theater
1 - 12
2 - 3
3 - 2
4 - 3
5 - 2
6 - 2
7 - 5
8 - 5

II-K Vaudeville
1 - 15
2 - 15
3 - 15
4 - 3

SECTION III
FAMOUS PEOPLE &
ORGANIZATIONS

III-A Boy Scouts
1 - 12
2 - 8
3 - 8
4 - 10
5 - 6
6 - 8
7 - 6
8 - 6
9 - 10
10 - 15
11 - 6
12 - 6
13 - 8
14 - 15
15 - 15
16 - 15
17 - 15
18 - 5
19 - 5
20 - 5
21 - 10
22 - 15
23 - 3
24 - 5
25 - 3

III-B Explorers
1 - 20
2 - 15
3 - 25
4 - 25

III-C Famous People
1 - 25
2 - 25
3 - 15
4 - 25
5 - 20
6 - 10
7 - 5
8 - 10
9 - 10
10 - 2
11 - 30

III-D Firemen
1 - 20
2 - 20
3 - 10
4 - 5
5 - 5
6 - 5
7 - 3
8 - 3
9 - 15
10 - 3
11 - 8
12 - 8
13 - 5
14 - 10
15 - 8
16 - 8
17 - 8
18 - 8

III-E Indians
1 - 5
2 - 3
3 - 5
4 - 6
5 - 5
6 - 3
7 - 8
8 - 5

III-F Nationality Heroes
1 - 20
2 - 8
3 - 2
4 - 30
5 - 5
6 - 5
7 - 5
8 - 10
9 - 3

10 - 5
11 - 30
12 - 5
13 - 10
14 - 10
15 - 3
16 - 3
17 - 3
18 - 3
19 - 3
20 - 3
21 - 3
22 - 3
23 - 4
24 - 50
25 - 15
26 - 8
27 - 3

III-G Organizations
1 - 5
2 - 20
3 - 2
4 - 15
5 - 3
6 - 3
7 - 1
8 - 15
9 - 1
10 - 2
11 - 2
12 - 2
13 - 2
14 - 2
15 - 10
16 - 2
17 - 2
18 - 10
19 - 2

III-H Religion
1 - 2
2 - 1
3 - 1
4 - 1
5 - 1
6 - 1
7 - 1
8 - 1

III-I Royal Families
1 - 15
2 - 10
3 - 10
4 - 10
5 - 6
6 - 6
7 - 8
8 - 6

9 - 5
10 - 5
11 - 8
12 - 4
13 - 6
14 - 6
15 - 6
16 - 10

SECTION IV
GEOGRAPHICAL
AREAS

IV-A Cities
1 - 5
2 - 10
3 - 10
4 - 2
5 - 2
6 - 2
7 - 6
8 - 3
9 - 3
10 - 10
11 - 10

IV-B Countries
1 - 2
2 - 2

IV-C Places
1 - 3
2 - 15
3 - 2
4 - 1
5 - 1
6 - 1
7 - 1
8 - 1

IV-D States
1 - 15
2 - 2
3 - 3
4 - 2
5 - 2
6 - 2
7 - 2
8 - 2

SECTION V
INSERT BUTTONS
IN SETS (Misc.)

V-A Gum Issues
1 - 2
2 - 2
3 - 2
4 - 4
5 - 4
6 - 4

V-B Tobacco Issues
1 - 2
2 - 6

V-C Issuer
Unknown
1 - 2
2 - 2
3 - 3

SECTION VI
MILITARY

VI-A Grand Army
of the Republic
1 - 5
2 - 12
3 - 12
4 - 6
5 - 8
6 - 4
7 - 6

VI-B Spanish-
American War
1 - 8
2 - 10
3 - 10
4 - 10
5 - 10
6 - 6
7 - 12
8 - 10
9 - 15
10 - 8
11 - 8
12 - 6
13 - 15
14 - 15
15 - 15
16 - 15
17 - 20
18 - 20
19 - 8
20 - 6

VI-C World War I
1 - 8
2 - 5
3 - 5
4 - 10
5 - 12
6 - 8
7 - 5
8 - 5
9 - 15
10 - 5

11 - 5
12 - 5
13 - 5
14 - 8
15 - 8
16 - 8
17 - 8
18 - 8
19 - 8
20 - 4
21 - 4
22 - 4
23 - 4
24 - 8
25 - 10
26 - 5
27 - 5
28 - 2
29 - 2
30 - 2
31 - 2
32 - 3
33 - 3
34 - 3
35 - 2
36 - 1
37 - 2
38 - 2
39 - 1
40 - 5
41 - 3
42 - 3
43 - 15
44 - 2
45 - 2
46 - 2
47 - 2

VI-D World War II
1 - 8
2 - 5
3 - 8
4 - 6
5 - 6
6 - 8
7 - 10
8 - 12
9 - 8
10 - 8
11 - 8
12 - 10
13 - 25
14 - 6
15 - 8
16 - 8
17 - 8
18 - 30

19 - 8
20 - 12
21 - 12
22 - 12
23 - 10
24 - 8
25 - 8
26 - 20
27 - 10
28 - 15
29 - 15
30 - 10
31 - 8
32 - 8
33 - 5
34 - 5
35 - 8
36 - 6
37 - 5
38 - 4
39 - 8
40 - 6
41 - 8
42 - 5
43 - 4
44 - 6
45 - 6
46 - 6
47 - 6
48 - 6
49 - 3
50 - 3
51 - 3
52 - 3
53 - 3
54 - 3
55 - 6
56 - 5
57 - 5
58 - 6
59 - 6
60 - 8
61 - 4
62 - 6
63 - 6
64 - 3
65 - 4
66 - 6
67 - 6
68 - 6
69 - 6
70 - 10
71 - 5
72 - 4
73 - 3
74 - 8

75 - 6
76 - 6
77 - 6
78 - 8
79 - 8
80 - 20
81 - 3
82 - 4
83 - 4
84 - 4
85 - 4
86 - 4
87 - 6
88 - 6
89 - 8
90 - 6
91 - 8
92 - 6
93 - 6
94 - 5
95 - 5
96 - 5
97 - 5
98 - 5
99 - 5
100 - 5
101 - 5
102 - 5
103 - 5
104 - 5
105 - 5
106 - 5
107 - 5
108 - 5
109 - 5
110 - 5
111 - 5
112 - 5
113 - 5

VI-E Vietnam War
1 - 3
2 - 3
3 - 3
4 - 3
5 - 3
6 - 3
7 - 3
8 - 3
9 - 3
10 - 3
11 - 2
12 - 2
13 - 2
14 - 2
15 - 2
16 - 2

VI-E Vietnam War
continued
17 - 2
18 - 3
19 - 3
20 - 4
21 - 5
22 - 3
23 - 3
24 - 3
25 - 3
26 - 3
27 - 2
28 - 2
29 - 3
30 - 2
31 - 2
32 - 2
33 - 2

**SECTION VII
PRODUCT &
SERVICE
ADVERTISING**

**VII-AL Alcoholic
Drinks**
1 - 12
2 - 6
3 - 12
4 - 4
5 - 10
6 - 4
7 - 4
8 - 8
9 - 6
10 - 12
11 - 12
12 - 12
13 - 8
14 - 6
15 - 6
16 - 10
17 - 4
18 - 4
19 - 12
20 - 10
21 - 12
22 - 5
23 - 5
24 - 4
25 - 4
26 - 4
27 - 8
28 - 5
29 - 4
30 - 5

31 - 3
32 - 3
33 - 3
34 - 3

**VII-AU Auto
Products & Clubs**
1 - 10
2 - 12
3 - 8
4 - 5
5 - 6
6 - 6
7 - 5
8 - 5
9 - 15
10 - 6
11 - 6
12 - 4
13 - 3
14 - 5
15 - 4
16 - 3
17 - 3
18 - 2
19 - 2

VII-BA Banks
1 - 15
2 - 10
3 - 3

VII-BO Boots
1 - 4
2 - 7
3 - 4
4 - 8

VII-BR Bread
1 - 6
2 - 6
3 - 15
4 - 8
5 - 8
6 - 10
7 - 4
8 - 5
9 - 4
10 - 12
11 - 4
12 - 15
13 - 10
14 - 3
15 - 8
16 - 5
17 - 2
18 - 2
19 - 5
20 - 2

21 - 2
22 - 4
23 - 3
24 - 8
25 - 3
26 - 4
27 - 4
28 - 2
29 - 12
30 - 4

**VII-BP Building
Products**
1 - 25
2 - 20
3 - 4
4 - 8
5 - 8
6 - 5
7 - 3

**VII-BM Business
Machines**
1 - 8
2 - 8
3 - 3
4 - 6
5 - 10
6 - 10
7 - 4
8 - 8
9 - 5
10 - 4
11 - 6

VII-BU Butter
1 - 12
2 - 5
3 - 3
4 - 2

**VII-BT Button
Manufacturers**
1 - 20
2 - 5
3 - 8
4 - 10
5 - 5
6 - 10
7 - 20
8 - 5

VII-CE Cereal
1 - 15
2 - 10
3 - 8
4 - 8
5 - 3
6 - 3
7 - 20
8 - 8

**VII-CA Cleaning
Agents**
1 - 15
2 - 10
3 - 5
4 - 20
5 - 30
6 - 15
7 - 10
8 - 8
9 - 5
10 - 6
11 - 5
12 - 4
13 - 15
14 - 8
15 - 3
16 - 4
17 - 4
18 - 4
19 - 3
20 - 8
21 - 8
22 - 6
23 - 3
24 - 6

VII-CL Clothing
1 - 25
2 - 8
3 - 8
4 - 15
5 - 25
6 - 8
7 - 5
8 - 5
9 - 8
10 - 6
11 - 3
12 - 15
13 - 12
14 - 6
15 - 3
16 - 3
17 - 2
18 - 10
19 - 2
20 - 2
21 - 10
22 - 3
23 - 2

VII-CO Coffee
1 - 15
2 - 15
3 - 12
4 - 12

VII-CO Coffee
continued
- 5 - 20
- 6 - 10
- 7 - 10
- 8 - 8
- 9 - 4
- 10 - 3
- 11 - 3
- 12 - 3
- 13 - 7
- 14 - 3
- 15 - 6
- 16 - 3
- 17 - 2
- 18 - 2
- 19 - 4
- 20 - 4
- 21 - 8
- 22 - 3
- 23 - 6
- 24 - 8

VII-DE Department Stores
- 1 - 5
- 2 - 4
- 3 - 4
- 4 - 5
- 5 - 5
- 6 - 3
- 7 - 6
- 8 - 3

VII-EL Electricity
- 1 - 3
- 2 - 12
- 3 - 3
- 4 - 4
- 5 - 3
- 6 - 5
- 7 - 2

VII-FA Farm Equipment
- 1 - 35
- 2 - 30
- 3 - 35
- 4 - 30
- 5 - 30
- 6 - 30
- 7 - 30
- 8 - 30
- 9 - 30
- 10 - 10
- 11 - 25
- 12 - 15
- 13 - 20
- 14 - 15

- 15 - 20
- 16 - 15
- 17 - 10
- 18 - 6
- 19 - 12
- 25 - 30
- 26 - 75
- 27 - 20
- 28 - 10
- 29 - 6
- 30 - 6
- 31 - 15
- 32 - 60
- 33 - 45
- 34 - 60
- 35 - 25
- 36 - 10
- 37 - 15
- 38 - 10
- 39 - 12
- 40 - 15
- 41 - 6
- 42 - 5
- 43 - 12
- 44 - 12
- 45 - 12
- 46 - 15
- 47 - 40
- 48 - 15
- 49 - 12
- 50 - 12
- 51 - 15
- 52 - 10
- 53 - 8
- 54 - 10
- 55 - 20
- 56 - 8
- 57 - 12
- 58 - 8
- 59 - 5
- 60 - 15
- 61 - 15
- 62 - 10
- 63 - 60
- 64 - 12
- 65 - 15
- 66 - 15
- 67 - 12
- 68 - 8
- 69 - 8
- 70 - 7
- 71 - 10
- 72 - 10
- 73 - 10
- 74 - 10
- 75 - 10
- 76 - 10
- 77 - 15
- 78 - 12

VII-FE Fertilizer
- 1 - 6
- 2 - 6
- 3 - 6
- 4 - 5

VII-FL Flour
- 1 - 12
- 2 - 8
- 3 - 18
- 4 - 6
- 5 - 4
- 6 - 8
- 7 - 4
- 8 - 8
- 9 - 3
- 10 - 8
- 11 - 5
- 12 - 15
- 13 - 5
- 14 - 3
- 15 - 4

VII-FO Foods Misc.
- 1 - 15
- 2 - 3
- 3 - 4
- 4 - 4
- 5 - 3
- 6 - 4
- 7 - 4
- 8 - 10
- 9 - 2
- 10 - 3
- 11 - 3
- 12 - 6
- 13 - 8
- 14 - 10
- 15 - 6
- 16 - 4
- 17 - 15
- 18 - 15
- 19 - 15
- 20 - 12
- 21 - 3
- 22 - 1
- 23 - 3
- 24 - 10
- 25 - 5
- 26 - 6
- 27 - 6
- 28 - 6
- 29 - 8
- 30 - 8
- 31 - 25
- 32 - 3
- 33 - 12

- 34 - 3
- 35 - 2
- 36 - 10
- 37 - 12
- 38 - 6
- 39 - 5
- 40 - 4
- 41 - 15
- 42 - 5
- 43 - 12
- 44 - 15

VII-FU Fuel
- 1 - 8
- 2 - 10
- 3 - 12
- 4 - 4
- 5 - 3
- 6 - 3
- 7 - 3
- 8 - 2
- 9 - 2
- 10 - 4
- 11 - 2
- 12 - 5

VII-GU Gun Powder
- 1 - 20
- 2 - 25
- 3 - 15
- 4 - 15
- 5 - 40
- 6 - 35
- 7 - 40
- 8 - 20

Dupont
- 9 - 25
- 10 - 20
- 11 - 20
- 12 - 15
- 13 - 6

Winchester
- 14 - 10
- 15 - 10
- 16 - 10
- 17 - 35
- 18 - 35

Ballistite & Empire
- 19 - 12
- 20 - 15
- 21 - 12
- 22 - 12

Remington UMC
- 23 - 25
- 24 - 25
- 25 - 25

**VII-GU Gun
Powder**
continued

26 - 30
27 - 35
28 - 15
29 - 12
30 - 12
31 - 10
32 - 12
33 - 15
34 - 15
Peters
35 - 20
36 - 25
37 - 15
38 - 25
39 - 25
40 - 25
41 - 20
42 - 15
43 - 20
44 - 15
45 - 15
46 - 15
47 - 20
48 - 30
49 - 15
50 - 15
51 - 12
52 - 12
53 - 15
54 - 10
Guns
55 - 35
56 - 35
57 - 35
58 - 30

**VII-HA Home
Appliances**
1 - 10
2 - 15
3 - 8
4 - 25
5 - 10
6 - 8
7 - 8
8 - 12
9 - 8
10 - 8
11 - 8
12 - 4
13 - 20
14 - 6
15 - 6
16 - 4
17 - 20
18 - 15
19 - 4
20 - 4

**VII-HF Home
Furnishings**
1 - 25
2 - 12
3 - 12
4 - 8
5 - 10
6 - 8

VII-HO Hosiery
1 - 10
2 - 10
3 - 8
4 - 35
5 - 10
6 - 10
7 - 10
8 - 10
9 - 6
10 - 10
11 - 6
12 - 10

VII-HT Hotels
1 - 8
2 - 5
3 - 3
4 - 5

VII-IC Ice Cream
1 - 30
2 - 8
3 - 5
4 - 2

VII-IN Insurance
1 - 8
2 - 15
3 - 6
4 - 2
5 - 5
6 - 5
7 - 4
8 - 4
9 - 4
10 - 4
11 - 4
12 - 4

**VII-LI Livestock &
Poultry**
1 - 35
2 - 15
3 - 8
4 - 10
5 - 10
6 - 30
7 - 8
8 - 8
9 - 8

10 - 8
11 - 12
12 - 5
13 - 8
14 - 8
15 - 5
16 - 5
17 - 4
18 - 4

**VII-LF Livestock &
Poultry Feed**
1 - 40
2 - 10
3 - 5
4 - 5
5 - 6
6 - 4
7 - 3
8 - 3

**VII-LM Livestock &
Poultry Medicine**
1 - 12
2 - 8
3 - 15
4 - 8
5 - 3
6 - 3
7 - 5
8 - 8

VII-MA Magazines
1 - 20
2 - 6
3 - 3
4 - 3

VII-MT Meat
1 - 40
2 - 15
3 - 8
4 - 6
5 - 8
6 - 5
7 - 5
8 - 5
9 - 5
10 - 5
11 - 8
12 - 4
13 - 8
14 - 8
15 - 8
16 - 8
17 - 3
18 - 5
19 - 5
20 - 4

VII-ME Medicine
1 - 60
2 - 20
3 - 10
4 - 15
5 - 15
6 - 15
7 - 60
8 - 35
9 - 35
10 - 6
11 - 6
12 - 6
13 - 8
14 - 20
15 - 4
16 - 3
17 - 3
18 - 3
19 - 2

VII-MI Milk
1 - 5
2 - 5
3 - 3
4 - 6
5 - 6
6 - 6
7 - 6
8 - 6
9 - 5
10 - 6
11 - 6
12 - 10
13 - 6
14 - 5
15 - 3
16 - 3
17 - 3
18 - 4
19 - 3

**VII-MU Musical
Instruments**
1 - 35
2 - 12
3 - 12
4 - 8
5 - 6
6 - 6
7 - 6
8 - 3
9 - 5
10 - 4
11 - 8
12 - 5

VII-NE Newspapers
1 - 20
2 - 10
3 - 10
4 - 5
5 - 3
6 - 2
7 - 3
8 - 5

VII-NA Non-Alcoholic Drinks
1 - 10
2 - 12
3 - 30
4 - 5
5 - 8
6 - 3
7 - 10
8 - 15
9 - 2
10 - 2
11 - 1
12 - 1
13 - 15
14 - 10
15 - 8
16 - 8
17 - 10
18 - 6
19 - 6
20 - 6
21 - 8
22 - 10
23 - 5
24 - 3

VII-PA Paint
1 - 8
2 - 8
3 - 8
4 - 6
5 - 8
6 - 5
7 - 3
8 - 5
9 - 3
10 - 3
11 - 2
12 - 2

VII-PH Phonographs
1 - 25
2 - 15
3 - 10

VII-PT Photography
1 - 15
2 - 20
3 - 20
4 - 30

VII-PR Product Advertising Misc.
1 - 4
2 - 6
3 - 6
4 - 20
5 - 8
6 - 5
7 - 5
8 - 5
9 - 4
10 - 3
11 - 5
12 - 4
13 - 8
14 - 8
15 - 10
16 - 12

VII-RE Real Estate
1 - 3
2 - 3
3 - 5
4 - 5
5 - 3
6 - 3
7 - 3

VII-RS Restaurants
1 - 3
2 - 3
3 - 3

VII-SE Service Advertising Misc.
1 - 3
2 - 3
3 - 3
4 - 3

VII-SH Shoes
1 - 60
2 - 50
3 - 10
4 - 10
5 - 20
6 - 15
7 - 12
8 - 8
9 - 15
10 - 10
11 - 20
12 - 15
13 - 30

14 - 10
15 - 8
16 - 8
17 - 6
18 - 6
19 - 4
20 - 6
21 - 8
22 - 5
23 - 8
24 - 4
25 - 8
26 - 8
27 - 3
28 - 4
29 - 3
30 - 3
31 - 3
32 - 6
33 - 8
34 - 8
35 - 4

VII-TE Telephones
1 - 15
2 - 8
3 - 8
4 - 8

VII-TO Tobacco
1 - 40
2 - 20
3 - 30
4 - 10
5 - 8
6 - 8
7 - 15
8 - 6
9 - 4
10 - 5
11 - 10
12 - 6
13 - 5
14 - 5
15 - 5
16 - 4

VII-TL Tools & Cutlery
1 - 30
2 - 8
3 - 6
4 - 6
5 - 3
6 - 5
7 - 3
8 - 3
9 - 6

VII-TY Toys
1 - 25
2 - 35
3 - 6
4 - 8
5 - 30
6 - 5
7 - 3
8 - 3
9 - 30
10 - 8
11 - 12
12 - 8
13 - 15
14 - 20
15 - 25
16 - 15
17 - 15
18 - 15
19 - 15
20 - 5

VII-TR Travel
1 - 3
2 - 2
3 - 3
4 - 3

VII-WA Watches
1 - 5
2 - 5
3 - 4
4 - 6
5 - 3
6 - 30

SECTION VIII PRESIDENTIAL CAMPAIGNS

1896-M William McKinley & Garret Hobart
1 - 50
2 - 15
3 - 20
4 - 20
5 - 12
6 - 8
7 - 8
8 - 8
9 - 8
10 - 10
11 - 8
12 - 8
13 - 8
14 - 6
15 - 8

McKinley & Hobart
continued
16 - 8
17 - 15
18 - 8
19 - 8
20 - 7
21 - 8
22 - 7
23 - 12
24 - 6

1896-B
William J. Bryan &
Arthur Sewall
1 - 25
2 - 25
3 - 15
4 - 15
5 - 50
6 - 20
7 - 20
8 - 100
9 - 12
10 - 15
11 - 20
12 - 7
13 - 6
14 - 65
15 - 35
16 - 5
17 - 15
18 - 15
19 - 15
20 - 15

1900-M
William McKinley &
Theodore Roosevelt
1 - 20
2 - 15
3 - 20
4 - 35
5 - 15
6 - 15
7 - 100
8 - 30
9 - 30
10 - 10
11 - 10
12 - 10

1900-B
William J. Bryan &
A.E. Stevenson
1 - 75
2 - 125
3 - 15

4 - 75
5 - 25
6 - 300
7 - 18
8 - 18
9 - 75
10 - 35
11 - 10
12 - 10
13 - 15
14 - 8
15 - 8

1904-R
Theodore Roosevelt
& Charles Fairbanks
1 - 35
2 - 35
3 - 40
4 - 75
5 - 12
6 - 60
7 - 75
8 - 12
9 - 12
10 - 30
11 - 12
12 - 10
13 - 7
14 - 18
15 - 12
16 - 10
17 - 8
18 - 6
19 - 6
20 - 10
21 - 6
22 - 6
23 - 5

1904-P
Alton Parker &
Henry Davis
1 - 20
2 - 35
3 - 20
4 - 25
5 - 85
6 - 50
7 - 20
8 - 15
9 - 20
10 - 20
11 - 20
12 - 30
13 - 30
14 - 20

15 - 20
16 - 15
17 - 20
18 - 20
19 - 20
20 - 20

1908-T
William Taft &
James Sherman
1 - 35
2 - 60
3 - 20
4 - 140
5 - 50
6 - 12
7 - 12
8 - 12
9 - 12
10 - 10
11 - 15
12 - 12
13 - 12
14 - 6
15 - 8
16 - 8
17 - 8
18 - 5
19 - 6
20 - 6

1908-B
William J. Bryan &
John Kern
1 - 85
2 - 150
3 - 150
4 - 30
5 - 100
6 - 30
7 - 50
8 - 20
9 - 45
10 - 90
11 - 40
12 - 40
13 - 40
14 - 40
15 - 75
16 - 15
17 - 20
18 - 12
19 - 15
20 - 60

1912-W
Woodrow Wilson &
Thomas Marshall
1 - 200
2 - 300
3 - 125
4 - 30

1912-T
William Taft &
James Sherman
1 - 50
2 - 12
3 - 10
4 - 8

1912-R
Theodore Roosevelt
& Hiram Johnson
1 - 450
2 - 40
3 - 12
4 - 20
5 - 15
6 - 5
7 - 10
8 - 12

1916-W
Woodrow Wilson &
Thomas Marshall
1 - 20
2 - 10
3 - 12
4 - 10

1916-H
Charles Hughes &
Charles Fairbanks
1 - 100
2 - 150
3 - 75
4 - 35
5 - 10
6 - 20
7 - 12
8 - 12
9 - 12
10 - 10
11 - 12
12 - 15
13 - 8
14 - 12
15 - 15
16 - 5

1920-H
Warren Harding &
Calvin Coolidge
1 - 500
2 - 400
3 - 65
4 - 200
5 - 20
6 - 75
7 - 7
8 - 7
9 - 22
10 - 25
11 - 20

1920-C
James Cox &
Franklin Roosevelt
1 - 2500
2 - 3500
3 - 75
4 - 85
5 - 35
6 - 25

1924-C
Calvin Coolidge &
Charles Dawes
1 - 175
2 - 175
3 - 35
4 - 20
5 - 20
6 - 30
7 - 25
8 - 60
9 - 90
10 - 15
11 - 15
12 - 30
13 - 8
14 - 10
15 - 15
16 - 8
17 - 4
18 - 8
19 - 8
20 - 8
21 - 15
22 - 15
23 - 10
24 - 20

1924-D
John Davis &
Charles Bryan
1 - 900
2 - 60
3 - 65

4 - 210
5 - 75
6 - 50
7 - 50
8 - 75
9 - 100
10 - 50
11 - 60
12 - 40
13 - 200
14 - 200
15 - 80
16 - 80

1924-L
Robert La Follette &
Burton Wheeler
1 - 60
2 - 30
3 - 30
4 - 12

1928-H
Herbert Hoover &
Charles Curtis
1 - 45
2 - 110
3 - 220
4 - 25
5 - 25
6 - 25
7 - 20
8 - 20
9 - 15
10 - 20
11 - 35
12 - 18
13 - 95
14 - 25
15 - 25
16 - 30
17 - 20
18 - 30
19 - 10
20 - 20
21 - 12
22 - 20
23 - 15

1928-S
Alfred Smith &
Joseph Robinson
1 - 500
2 - 95
3 - 60
4 - 75
5 - 285
6 - 40
7 - 65

8 - 35
9 - 35
10 - 20
11 - 15
12 - 10
13 - 60
14 - 135
15 - 25
16 - 50
17 - 50
18 - 25
19 - 40
20 - 25
21 - 15
22 - 15
23 - 15
24 - 25

1932-R
Franklin Roosevelt
& John Garner
1 - 500
2 - 250
3 - 6
4 - 9
5 - 18
6 - 15
7 - 70
8 - 25
9 - 60
10 - 175
11 - 12
12 - 8
13 - 14
14 - 12
15 - 10
16 - 15
17 - 7
18 - 10
19 - 8
20 - 25
21 - 7
22 - 5
23 - 2
24 - 2

1932-H
Herbert Hoover &
Charles Curtis
1 - 150
2 - 165
3 - 210
4 - 75
5 - 180
6 - 8
7 - 14
8 - 34
9 - 30

10 - 18
11 - 22
12 - 9
13 - 12
14 - 7
15 - 18
16 - 9
17 - 22
18 - 17
19 - 8
20 - 8
21 - 6
22 - 8
23 - 8

1936-R
Franklin Roosevelt
& John Garner
1 - 10
2 - 200
3 - 24
4 - 35
5 - 15
6 - 50
7 - 10
8 - 25
9 - 6
10 - 16
11 - 9
12 - 10
13 - 6
14 - 2
15 - 5
16 - 7
17 - 5
18 - 5
19 - 5
20 - 2
21 - 4
22 - 6
23 - 2
24 - 5

1936-L
Alfred Landon &
Franklin Knox
1 - 50
2 - 500
3 - 60
4 - 6
5 - 10
6 - 100
7 - 15
8 - 15
9 - 130
10 - 20
11 - 10

Landon & Knox
continued
12 - 50
13 - 16
14 - 15
15 - 20
16 - 40
17 - 22
18 - 16
19 - 15
20 - 14
21 - 7
22 - 12
23 - 7
24 - 5

1940-R
Franklin Roosevelt
& Henry Wallace
1 - 12
2 - 10
3 - 70
4 - 60
5 - 6
6 - 8
7 - 10
8 - 18
9 - 18
10 - 10
11 - 4
12 - 6
13 - 85
14 - 65
15 - 9
16 - 30
17 - 3
18 - 3
19 - 3
20 - 3
21 - 3
22 - 3
23 - 3
24 - 3

1940-W
Wendell Willkie &
Charles McNary
1 - 60
2 - 50
3 - 38
4 - 24
5 - 4
6 - 5
7 - 5
8 - 5
9 - 3
10 - 60

11 - 7
12 - 3
13 - 3
14 - 6
15 - 90
16 - 3
17 - 12
18 - 30
19 - 17

1944-R
Franklin Roosevelt
& Harry Truman
1 - 40
2 - 30
3 - 14
4 - 8
5 - 6
6 - 4
7 - 6
8 - 5
9 - 6
10 - 5
11 - 4
12 - 25
13 - 22
14 - 4
15 - 3
16 - 5
17 - 9
18 - 3
19 - 6

1944-D
Thomas Dewey &
John Bricker
1 - 150
2 - 45
3 - 3
4 - 15
5 - 9
6 - 6
7 - 13
8 - 5
9 - 4
10 - 10
11 - 8
12 - 7
13 - 12
14 - 2
15 - 3
16 - 3

1948-T
Harry Truman &
Alben Barkley
1 - 90
2 - 55
3 - 75
4 - 250
5 - 225
6 - 8
7 - 8
8 - 20
9 - 6
10 - 6
11 - 8
12 - 8
13 - 50
14 - 12
15 - 5
16 - 35
17 - 10
18 - 7
19 - 25
20 - 16

1948-D
Thomas Dewey &
Earl Warren
1 - 55
2 - 65
3 - 10
4 - 10
5 - 3
6 - 3
7 - 5
8 - 9
9 - 40
10 - 7
11 - 8

1948-TH
Strom Thurmond &
Fielding Wright
1 - 10
2 - 10

1952-E
Dwight Eisenhower
& Richard Nixon
1 - 85
2 - 7
3 - 10
4 - 5
5 - 7
6 - 8
7 - 3
8 - 12
9 - 4
10 - 4

11 - 4
12 - 3
13 - 3
14 - 4
15 - 3
16 - 8
17 - 3
18 - 4
19 - 4
20 - 50

1952-S
Adlai Stevenson &
John Sparkman
1 - 12
2 - 3
3 - 3
4 - 50
5 - 8
6 - 8
7 - 5
8 - 4
9 - 8
10 - 15
11 - 5
12 - 8
13 - 8
14 - 12
15 - 3
16 - 4
17 - 4
18 - 5
19 - 3
20 - 4

1956-E
Dwight Eisenhower
& Richard Nixon
1 - 60
2 - 4
3 - 5
4 - 3
5 - 4
6 - 4
7 - 5
8 - 4
9 - 3
10 - 3
11 - 3
12 - 2
13 - 5
14 - 3
15 - 2
16 - 10
17 - 2
18 - 1
19 - 1

**Eisenhower &
Nixon**
continued
20 - 1
21 - 1
22 - 1
23 - 1
24 - 2

**1956-S
Adlai Stevenson &
Estes Kefauver**
1 - 15
2 - 20
3 - 2
4 - 5
5 - 10
6 - 3
7 - 4
8 - 10
9 - 15
10 - 5
11 - 8
12 - 15
13 - 5
14 - 2
15 - 5
16 - 3
17 - 4
18 - 4

**1960-K
John Kennedy &
Lyndon Johnson**
1 - 6
2 - 6
3 - 20
4 - 2
5 - 2
6 - 2
7 - 3
8 - 60
9 - 2
10 - 2
11 - 2
12 - 2
13 - 2
14 - 2
15 - 2
16 - 15
17 - 8
18 - 7
19 - 4
20 - 4
21 - 3
22 - 5
23 - 2
24 - 2

**1960-N
Richard Nixon &
Henry Lodge**
1 - 4
2 - 75
3 - 5
4 - 3
5 - 8
6 - 4
7 - 4
8 - 8
9 - 4
10 - 3
11 - 2
12 - 2
13 - 2
14 - 4
15 - 4
16 - 11
17 - 2
18 - 2
19 - 2
20 - 2
21 - 2
22 - 2
23 - 2
24 - 2

**1964-J
Lyndon Johnson &
Hubert Humphrey**
1 - 4
2 - 3
3 - 2
4 - 2
5 - 2
6 - 2
7 - 14
8 - 3
9 - 3
10 - 4
11 - 3
12 - 2
13 - 2
14 - 2
15 - 1
16 - 1
17 - 1
18 - 3
19 - 1
20 - 1
21 - 2
22 - 1
23 - 3
24 - 2

**1964-G
Barry Goldwater &
William Miller**
1 - 4
2 - 3
3 - 4
4 - 2
5 - 2
6 - 2
7 - 2
8 - 5
9 - 2
10 - 1
11 - 2
12 - 2
13 - 2
14 - 4
15 - 2
16 - 2
17 - 2
18 - 4
19 - 2

**1968-N
Richard Nixon &
Spiro Agnew**
1 - 2
2 - 1
3 - .50
4 - 5
5 - 1
6 - 3
7 - 2
8 - 1
9 - 1
10 - 2
11 - 2
12 - .50
13 - .50

**1968-H
Hubert Humphrey
& Edmund Muskie**
1 - 3
2 - 3
3 - 3
4 - 3
5 - 4
6 - 2

**1968-W
George Wallace &
Curtis LeMay**
1 - 2
2 - 3
3 - 2
4 - 2
5 - 2
6 - 1
7 - 1

**1972-H
Hopefuls of all
Parties**
1 - 1
2 - 1
3 - .50
4 - 2
5 - 1
6 - 1
7 - 1
8 - .50
9 - .50
10 - 1
11 - .50
12 - .50
13 - .50
14 - 1
15 - 1
16 - .50
17 - 1
18 - 1

**SECTION IX
SOCIAL &
POLITICAL CAUSES**

**IX-A Animal
Welfare**
1 - 8
2 - 3
3 - 3
4 - 3

IX-B Civil Rights
1 - 6
2 - 5
3 - 8
4 - 3
5 - 2
6 - 2
7 - 1
8 - 2
9 - 2
10 - 2
11 - 2
12 - 30
13 - 2
14 - 2
15 - 2
16 - 10
17 - 5
18 - 3
19 - 5
20 - 5
21 - 5
22 - 2
23 - 2
24 - 2

IX-C Communist Party
1 - 10
2 - 8
3 - 6
4 - 3

IX-D Health
1 - 5
2 - 5
3 - 2
4 - 2
5 - 2
6 - 1
7 - 1
8 - 5
9 - 4
10 - 10
11 - 3
12 - 2
13 - 1
14 - 2
15 - 1
16 - 1

IX-E Humanitarian Relief
1 - 10
2 - 5
3 - 8
4 - 4
5 - 8
6 - 4
7 - 4
8 - 8
9 - 25
10 - 8
11 - 4
12 - 4
13 - 3
14 - 5
15 - 5
16 - 5
17 - 5
18 - 5
19 - 5
20 - 5
21 - 6
22 - 2
23 - 2

COLOR INSERT SECTION

VII-CE7 - 20
VII-FL9 - 3
VII-FO43 - 12
VII-TO14 - 5
XI-C26 - 5

VII-CA13 - 15
VII-HA20 - 4
VII-FL10 - 8
VII-CA14 - 8
VII-CA15 - 3
VII-FO4 - 4
VII-FO21 - 3
VII-FO2 - 3
VII-PT3 - 20
VII-CA16 - 4
VII-TO16 - 4
VII-PT4 - 30
VII-CA17 - 4
II-J8 - 5
VII-FL11 - 5
VII-FO29 - 8
VII-FL12 - 15
VII-FL13 - 5
VII-TO15 - 5
VII-GU35 - 20
VII-GU17 - 35
VII-GU25 - 25
VII-TL9 - 6
III-F24 - 50
III-F-25 - 15
VI-C43 - 15
XI-A20 - 35
VII-NA13 - 15
VII-CO13 - 7
VII-CO10 - 3
VII-FO36 - 10
VII-FA16 - 15
VII-FA59 - 5
III-D9 - 15
VII-TO13 - 5
VII-LM8 - 8
IV-D3 - 3
VII-FL8 - 8
VII-FO1 - 15
VII-HO9 - 6
II-C59 - 6
XI-J4 - 10
IX-D10 - 10
VII-FA71 - 10
VII-NA1 - 10
VII-MT1 - 40
VII-FL1 - 12
VII-GU1 - 20
VII-GU4 - 15
VII-FL2 - 8
VII-NE1 - 20
VII-TL1 - 40
II-C50 - 20
VI-B18 - 20
VI-C6 - 6

VII-LM1 - 12
VII-PR4 - 20
I-A5 - 12
XII-D2 - 15
III-F1 - 20
VII-BR3 - 15
VII-ME1 - 60
III-G2 - 20
I-A6 - 12
I-A3 - 20
I-A2 - 20
VII-PT1 - 15
II-C44 - 15
II-F4 - 15
II-A4 - 35

SECTION IX
continued

IX-F Labor
1 - 5
2 - 5
3 - 8
4 - 5
5 - 8
6 - 3
7 - 8
8 - 3
9 - 2
10 - 2
11 - 1
12 - 1

IX-G N.R.A.
1 - 3
2 - 5
3 - 5
4 - 5
5 - 5
6 - 2
7 - 3
8 - 5

IX-H Peace
1 - 4
2 - 5
3 - 3
4 - 4
5 - 4
6 - 4
7 - 4
8 - 4
9 - 8
10 - 10
11 - 4
12 - 4

IX-I Prohibition
1 - 20
2 - 5
3 - 6
4 - 5
5 - 20
6 - 8
7 - 5
8 - 10

IX-J Socialist Party
1 - 75
2 - 6
3 - 6
4 - 6

IX-K Tobacco
1 - 10
2 - 10
3 - 12
4 - 5
5 - 1

IX-L Women's Suffrage
1 - 12
2 - 20
3 - -12
4 - 10

SECTION X SPORTS

X-A Baseball
1 - 18
2 - 6
3 - 4
4 - 2
5 - 60
6 - 5
7 - 5
8 - 6
9 - 10
10 - 10
11 - 5
12 - 4
13 - 30
14 - 10
15 - 10
16 - 25
17 - 10
18 - 30
19 - 10
20 - 15
21 - 15
22 - 12
23 - 3
24 - 12
25 - 5
26 - 5

X-A Baseball
continued
27 - 4
28 - 12
29 - 8
30 - 8
31 - 6
32 - 6
33 - 6
34 - 6
35 - 6

X-B Boxing
1 - 15
2 - 30
3 - 12
4 - 20
5 - 12
6 - 8
7 - 8
8 - 5
9 - 3

X-C Sports Misc.
1 - 3
2 - 3
3 - 3
4 - 2
5 - 15
6 - 8
7 - 4
8 - 3
9 - 15
10 - 4
11 - 2
12 - 3
13 - 2
14 - 2
15 - 2
16 - 3
17 - 3
18 - 3
19 - 3
20 - 3
21 - 5
22 - 5
23 - 2

SECTION XI
TRANSPORTATION
& SPACE FLIGHT

XI-A Airplanes
1 - 8
2 - 10
3 - 8
4 - 8
5 - 8
6 - 12

7 - 8
8 - 8
9 - 8
10 - 3
11 - 3
12 - 3
13 - 5
14 - 15
15 - 12
16 - 15
17 - 15
18 - 8
19 - 30
20 - 35
21 - 8
22 - 10
23 - 12
24 - 30
25 - 30
26 - 12
27 - 8
28 - 12
29 - 10
30 - 4
31 - 3
32 - 90
33 - 20
34 - 35
35 - 25
36 - 20
37 - 18
38 - 15
39 - 20
40 - 15
41 - 15
42 - 15
43 - 25
44 - 10
45 - 20
46 - 20
47 - 20
48 - 20
49 - 20
50 - 30
51 - 15
52 - 40
53 - 15
54 - 15

XI-B Autos
1 - 30
2 - 10
3 - 8
4 - 8
5 - 10
6 - 8

7 - 20
8 - 10
9 - 8
10 - 10
11 - 6
12 - 8
13 - 8
14 - 8
15 - 8
16 - 8
17 - 6
18 - 8
19 - 8
20 - 8
21 - 7
22 - 7
23 - 6
24 - 6
25 - 8
26 - 8
27 - 20
28 - 2
29 - 8
30 - 8
31 - 8
32 - 3
33 - 25
34 - 15
35 - 5
36 - 8
37 - 8
38 - 12
39 - 12
40 - 12
41 - 15
42 - 15
43 - 12
44 - 6
45 - 8
46 - 5
47 - 8
48 - 30
49 - 35
50 - 10
51 - 10
52 - 20
53 - 20
54 - 8
55 - 6
56 - 8
57 - 8
58 - 12
59 - 35
60 - 6

61 - 8
62 - 5
63 - 6
64 - 6
65 - 8
66 - 5
67 - 10
68 - 8
69 - 8
70 - 12
71 - 8
72 - 8
73 - 8
74 - 8
75 - 8
76 - 8
77 - 10
78 - 6
79 - 12
80 - 10
81 - 8
82 - 6
83 - 5
84 - 8
85 - 15

XI-C Bicycles
1 - 8
2 - 10
3 - 10
4 - 12
5 - 12
6 - 12
7 - 10
8 - 8
9 - 12
10 - 8
11 - 8
12 - 8
13 - 15
14 - 8
15 - 8
16 - 8
17 - 8
18 - 8
19 - 6
20 - 6
21 - 10
22 - 6
23 - 5
24 - 5
25 - 10
26 - 5
27 - 5
28 - 5
29 - 10

XI-C Bicycles
continued
30 - 5
31 - 5
32 - 8
33 - 8
34 - 10
35 - 8
36 - 8
37 - 6
38 - 5
39 - 10
40 - 5
41 - 5
42 - 8
43 - 8
44 - 5

XI-D Boats
1 - 2
2 - 5
3 - 5
4 - 4

XI-E Carriages
1 - 20
2 - 8
3 - 12
4 - 5
5 - 10
6 - 10
7 - 10

XI-F Motorcycles
1 - 15
2 - 25
3 - 25
4 - 5
5 - 20
6 - 15
7 - 15
8 - 8

XI-G Railroads
1 - 15
2 - 8
3 - 20
4 - 4
5 - 3
6 - 6
7 - 4
8 - 3
9 - 4
10 - 3
11 - 2
12 - 3
13 - 3

XI-H Ships
1 - 3
2 - 3
3 - 3
4 - 3
5 - 8
6 - 3
7 - 5
8 - 3

XI-I Space Flight
1 - 3
2 - 3
3 - 10
4 - 5
5 - 3
6 - 3
7 - 3

XI-J Subways & Trolleys
1 - 5
2 - 5
3 - 5
4 - 10
5 - 3
6 - 5
7 - 3

SECTION XII WORLD'S FAIRS

XII-A Trans-Mississippi 1898
1 - 10
2 - 12
3 - 12
4 - 12

XII-B Pan American 1901
1 - 15
2 - 10
3 - 15
4 - 8
5 - 12
6 - 15

XII-C St. Louis 1904
1 - 18
2 - 12
3 - 8
4 - 6
5 - 6
6 - 15
7 - 6
8 - 6
9 - 10
10 - 6
11 - 5

XII-D Lewis & Clark 1905
1 - 25
2 - 15

XII-E Jamestown 1907
1 - 15
2 - 10
3 - 8
4 - 5

XII-F Alaska-Yukon-Pacific 1909
1 - 30
2 - 5
3 - 5

XII-G Hudson-Fulton 1909
1 - 8
2 - 5
3 - 5

XII-H Panama-California 1915
1 - 15
2 - 6
3 - 5
4 - 6

XII-I Panama-Pacific 1915
1 - 6
2 - 6
3 - 6

XII-J Sesquicen-tennial 1926
1 - 6
2 - 5
3 - 5
4 - 4

XII-K Century of Progress 1933
1 - 8
2 - 8
3 - 15
4 - 6
5 - 5
6 - 5
7 - 5
8 - 5
9 - 5
10 - 4
11 - 5
12 - 5

XII-L Golden Gate 1939
1 - 6
2 - 6
3 - 4

XII-M New York 1939
1 - 4
2 - 4
3 - 4
4 - 4
5 - 6
6 - 4
7 - 4
8 - 4
9 - 8
10 - 8
11 - 8
12 - 8
13 - 8
14 - 6
15 - 8
16 - 4

XII-N Seattle 1961
1 - 3
2 - 3

XII-O New York 1964
1 - 3
2 - 3
3 - 2

XII-P Expo 67
1 - 2
2 - 2
3 - 2

REFERENCE BOOKS
FOR COLLECTORS

All prices include "bookrate" postage. For faster delivery via U.P.S. add $1.00 for the first book and 50¢ for each additional book. For U.P.S. provide a street address. Pennsylvania residents add 6% sales tax.

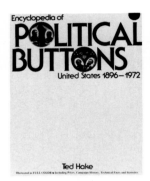

1

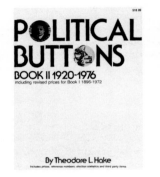

2

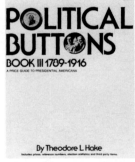

3

PLEASE NOTE: The above three books are companion volumes covering all presidential elections from 1789 through 1976. There is no duplication. Together they illustrate and evaluate over 12,000 presidential campaign collectibles.

4

5

HAKE'S
MAIL BID
AUCTIONS
& SALES
CATALOGUES

6

1. ENCYCLOPEDIA OF POLITICAL BUTTONS 1896-1972 (BOOK I). A *full-color* price guide picturing 4,000 presidential campaign buttons and novelty items. Includes election histories and statistics for each campaign. Each item has its own code number used by collectors to identify their items and communicate with other collectors. Recognized as an indispensible reference since its publication in 1974 and the only full-color price guide on presidential Americana. A revised price supplement that provides up to date evaluations for each of the 4000 items comes with each book.

8½ x 11", 256 pages   **Softbound $21.50**

2. POLITICAL BUTTONS BOOK II 1920-1976. This book prices and pictures in black & white 4000 additional buttons and related presidential campaign items *not* included in Book I. Campaigns from 1952 through 1976 are covered more thoroughly in this book than in Book I. Complete election statistics are included and each item has a code number to facilitate communication among collectors. Recognized in the hobby as an essential reference work.

8½ x 11", 256 pages   **Softbound $19.50**
                                                             Hardbound $26.50

3. POLITICAL BUTTONS BOOK III 1789-1916. The finest collections throughout the country were photographed to assemble this remarkable record of American political history since George Washington's era. The book prices and pictures in black & white 4000 presidential campaign items such as portrait badges, ribbons, textiles, tokens, posters, china, canes, mechanical novelties, flags, ferrotype and cardboard badges, celluloid badges and many other unusual campaign collectibles. Complete election statistics are included and each item has a code number. This is the first and only comprehensive reference work on presidential campaign artifacts of the 19th century.

8½ x 11", 256 pages   **Softbound $19.50**
                                                             Hardbound $26.50

4. THE BUTTON BOOK. The only book devoted to all types of pinback buttons issued since 1896. There is a small section on presidential buttons but the main emphasis is on the beautifully designed pinbacks used to advertise products of all types, publicize comic characters and movies, commemorate events, wars, expositions, etc., and depict heroes from baseball stars to Lindbergh. This book will delight anyone interested in history or graphics. **BUTTONS IN SETS** updates the values and sets of buttons that were originally in **THE BUTTON BOOK.** Our supply of **THE BUTTON BOOK** is very limited. A totally new second volume is planned.

6 x 9", 256 pages   **Hardbound $21.50**

5. SIX GUN HEROES: A PRICE GUIDE TO MOVIE COWBOY COLLECTIBLES by Hake and Robert D. Cauler. Another standard reference for the field. Over 500 examples of character collectibles are pictured plus biographies and filmographies for Hopalong Cassidy, Roy Rogers, The Lone Ranger, Tom Mix, Gene Autry, and other Western heroes.

8½ x 11", 140 pages   **Softbound $11.50**

6. HAKE'S MAIL BID AUCTION/IMMEDIATE SALE CATALOGUES. Completely illustrated catalogues are issued quarterly offering approximately 2000 items. Over 100 collecting categories are represented with emphasis on comic character items, Disneyana, toys, movies, premiums, TV items, paperdolls, Western and space heroes, political items, advertising collectibles, transportation, expositions, wars, Boy Scouts, baseball, and pinback buttons of all types. A sample copy is available for $2.00 from Hake's Americana & Collectibles, P.O. Box 1444, York, PA 17405.

INDEX